To

Peter Schleger

My Very Warmest

Regards

Craig Way 1/3/2004

GLENN MILLER
IN BRITAIN
THEN AND NOW

Chris Way

*The real enjoyment comes from the moments inside our work.
Once we heard the happy sound of a music-hungry bunch of
servicemen, yelling for more whatever we had to offer, we knew that
we could never enjoy a more satisfying pay-off in our lives.*

GLENN MILLER, SEPTEMBER 14, 1944

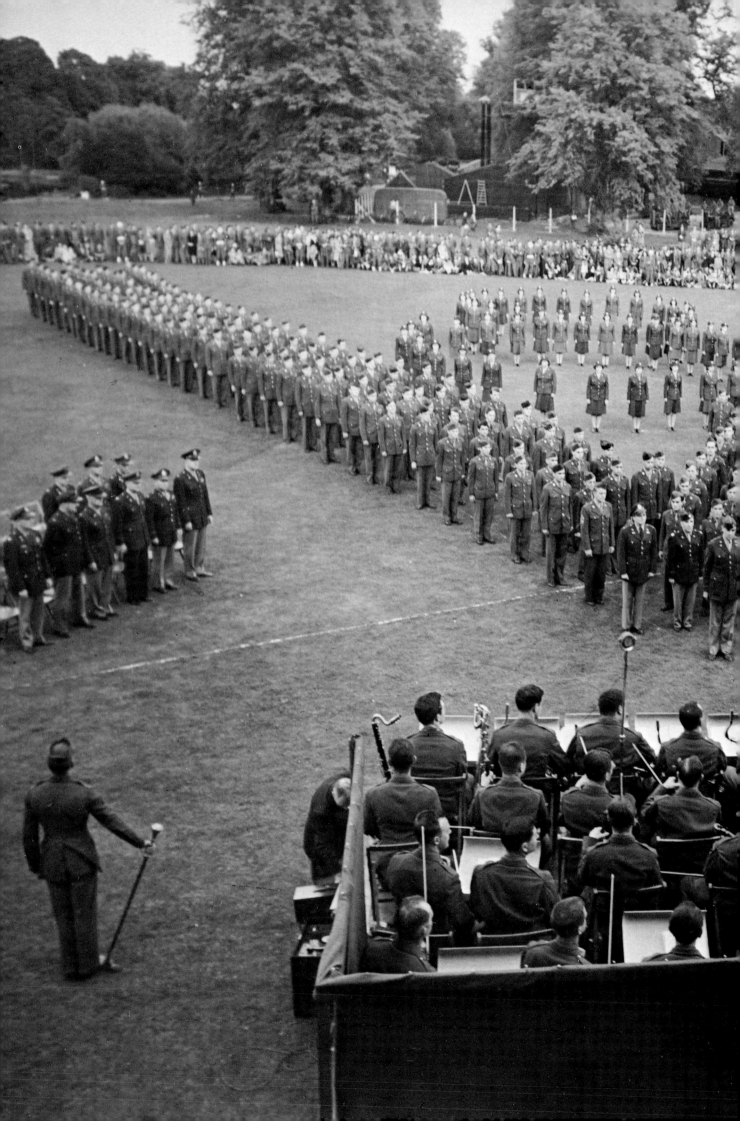

GLENN MILLER
IN BRITAIN
THEN AND NOW

Credits

© Chris Way and *After the Battle*
ISBN: 0 900913 92 4
Printed in Great Britain
Edited by Winston G. Ramsey
Designed by Gordon Ramsey
An *After the Battle* publication

PUBLISHERS
Battle of Britain Prints
International Ltd
Church House, Church Street,
London E15 3JA, England

PRINTERS
Plaistow Press Ltd
Church House, Church Street,
London E15 3JA, England

DEDICATION
Steven D. Miller, Jonnie Miller, Edward F. Polic, Connie Richards, and my dear father, Bernard Way.

FRONT COVER
Glenn Miller leads the trombone section of the American Band of the Allied Expeditionary Force at the High Wycombe concert held at the Eighth Air Force headquarters on July 29, 1944. (Painting by George A. Campbell)

BACK COVER
Major Vic Warzinski of the USAF at Mildenhall, Suffolk, and Jim Schoenecker, the Superintendent of the American Military Cemetery at Madingley (where Glenn Miller's name is commemorated on the Wall of the Missing), lay a wreath on the 50th anniversary of Miller's disappearance. (© The Telegraph plc, London, 1994)

FRONT ENDPAPER
The American Band of the AEF plays Halesworth — one of the three concerts given by the band on Sunday, August 6, 1944.

REAR ENDPAPER
Glenn and the band at the Abbey Road Studios on Saturday, September 16, 1944. Recordings took up an increasing part of the orchestra's time, particularly after the airfield concerts ceased in October.

FRONTISPIECE
The American Band of the Supreme Allied Command, directed by Captain Glenn Miller, at the headquarters of the Eighth Air Force in High Wycombe on Saturday, July 29, 1944. The occasion was the launch of the 'V-8' War Bond rally by General James H. Doolittle. The band would soon change its name to the one by which it is more popularly known: the American Band of the Allied Expeditionary Force.

PHOTOGRAPHS
Unless credited to the contrary, all contemporary photographs are from the author's collection. All present-day comparison photographs by *After the Battle* or its contributors.

Author's Acknowledgements

As is customary with an undertaking of this nature, thanks are due to many individuals and organisations for help and advice. First and foremost, I must express my sincere appreciation to the following people without whose time and efforts this book would not have materialised: Steven D. Miller, Glenn Miller's son; Gordon Richards; Mrs Connie Richards; Edward F. Polic; Martin Benge, Vice-President of EMI; Stephen Woolford, Education and Exhibits Officer at the Imperial War Museum, Duxford; Richard Harries and Stan Bruce.

A special note of thanks must go to Steve Miller and the Miller Estate for authorising the use of Glenn Miller's name in the title of this book.

Others who have helped are as follows: John Abrahams; David Ades; John Archer; Phillip Arnold; Mary Beth Barnard; Mr B. A. Bennett; Bob Braithwaite; Gloria Brent; Alan Brown; Colette Byatt of the American Air Museum in Britain; Paul Cannon of the Newbury Museum; Steve Casely; Colonel Paul Chryst, USAF; Arthur L. Clamp; Alison Coates, manager of The Corn Exchange, Newbury; Ray and Peggy Convine; Ray Corby; Bing Crosby; David Crow; Wallace Dahl; Alan Dann; Nigel Dawe; Alan Dell; Gerry Didymus; Wilfred Dimsdale; General James Doolittle, USAF; Paul Dudley; John Duffell; Denis Duffield; Ken Everett, Robert Farnon; Aldon Ferguson; Roger Freeman; Royal Frey; Ray Funnell; Norman Goodchild; Jack Green; Paula Green; John Hadfield; David Hale; Cliff Hall; Eric Hamilton; Rachel Hanson, Publicity Officer, De Montfort Hall; Evan Harris; Flight Lieutenant Jim Hathaway, RAF; Chris Hayes; Don Haynes; Ted Heath; Ian Henderson; James Hotaling; Margaret Hubble; Michael 'Peanuts' Hucko; Ted Inman, Director of the Imperial War Museum, Duxford; Vic Jenkins; David Johnson; Bill King; Pat Kirkwood; Des Lavers; Douglas Le-Vicki; Harry Long; Cecil Madden, MBE; Bill Manley; Richard C. March; Linda Marr; Ian McCloughlin, *Newbury Weekly News;* Ray McKinley; John Measures; Tony Middleton; Stephen Miles; Herb Miller; Jimmy Miller; John Miller; Jonnie Miller (Glenn Miller's daughter); Irene Miller-Woolfe; John Mills; Bobbie Mitchell, BBC Photo Library; Mike Morris; Peter Newbrook; Les Newport; Katie Page, Grantham Museum; Ray Paice; Nat Peck; Brian Prior; Bernie Priven; John Quinn; ex-President Ronald Reagan; Ivor R. Richmond; Mickey Russell; Steve Sandland; Larry Semmel; Anne Shelton MBE; Dinah Shore; Paul Southerington; George Stebbings; Marum Talbott; Roland Taylor, Chairman of the Glenn Miller Society; Tony Tichmarsh; Trixie Tracy; Colonel Upstrom USAF Museum; Brian Vincent; George Voutsas; Mike Warner; Robert Warren; John Watson; Ken Wells; James Wiseman; Nick Woodhead, *Grantham Journal;* John Woolnough;

Thanks are also due to the following organisations: the Royal Air Force; the United States Air Force; the 8th Air Force Historial Society; EMI/HMV Abbey Road Studios; the management of the Mount Royal Hotel; the management of the Prince Edward Theatre; the management of Kettner's Restaurant; the management of the Corn Exchange, Bedford; Bedford Borough Council; the Glenn Miller Society; the Miller Estate; the BBC Photographic Library; Hulton Deutsch Collection Ltd; *Bedfordshire Times*; *Melody Maker*; *Western Morning News*; *Grantham Journal; Newbury Weekly News; Leicester Mercury; Belfast Telegraph;* Eastern Counties Newspapers Ltd, Charles Wells Brewery; Boots PLC; Westminster Bank; Anglia Television; 4th Estate Productions; Grantham Museum; the Herb Miller Orchestra — Miller Magic; the Glenn Miller (UK) Orchestra; Richard Kallas Photography; The Royal British Legion (Bedford Branch); the residents of Melchbourne Park; Newbury District Museum; the management of De Montfort Hall; the United States Air Force Museum, Dayton, Ohio; the American Air Museum In Britain and the Imperial War Museum, Duxford.

PHOTO CREDITS

Aerofilms: 53 bottom.
G. I. Barnett & Son Ltd: 20 top.
BBC Photo Library: 25 centre and bottom, 80 top.
Bedford Newspapers: 129 bottom.
Bedfordshire Record Office: 22 middle, 25 top, 30 top left.
95th Bomb Group Archives: 56
100th Bomb Group Archives: 125 top and bottom right, 126 top.
392nd Bomb Group Archives: 135 top.
Brooks Photographic: 12 bottom, 130 bottom, 131 top left.
Alan Brown: 103.
Vic Brown: 35 top right.
Steve Casely: 110 bottom right, 111 bottom, 112 centre and bottom right, 113 bottom right.
Crown Copyright via RAF Museum: 19 bottom, 34 middle, 35 middle, 38 bottom right, 43 bottom right, 46 bottom, 49 top, 50 bottom, 52 middle, 57 top, 58 bottom, 60 centre left, 63 bottom right, 64 top, 96 bottom right, 100 bottom, 105 bottom, 114 bottom, 116 top, 124 bottom, 125 bottom left, 127 centre, 128 centre, 131 bottom, 134 bottom, 135 centre.
Nigel Dawe: 55 centre left, 107 all.
Devon County Council: 113 bottom left
Paul Dudley via Steve Miller: 64 centre.
Aldon Ferguson: 36 bottom right, 37 middle right and bottom right.
Glenn Miller Society: 110 bottom left.
Paula Green: 46 top.
Don Haynes: 67 centre left.
HMV/EMI: 78 top and bottom left, 79 top and bottom left.
Jack Hole: 99 bottom.
Hulton Deutsch: 26 bottom, 75 top left, 81 centre.
Imperial War Museum, Duxford: 39 top, 60 top, 130 bottom.
Imperial War Museum: 71 top, 74 top, 76 top.
Frank Ippolito: 21 top left and bottom left.
Colonel Isbell/USAF: 117 top.
Vic Jenkins: 104 top, 105 top

Bill King: 40 centre and bottom, 41 all, 99 bottom right.
Vic Knight Jr: 67 bottom left.
Carlo Krahmer: 84 top.
Louis Lawrence: 30 bottom.
Leicestershire County Council: 65 top.
Joe Loss: 37 top right.
Joe Luck: 138 top.
Cecil Madden: 70 bottom.
Richard March: 153 bottom.
Jack Marshall: 28 bottom, 73 centre left.
Ray McKinley: 133 centre left.
Melody Maker: 72 top, 87 top left.
Miller Estate: 80 bottom left, 87 top right.
Art Nanas: 140 bottom left.
National Monuments Record Service: 69 top, 76 bottom left, 81 top left.
Newbury District Museum: 99 centre.
Les Newport: 47 top left and right.
North West Heritage Group/British Aerospace: 132 top and bottom, 133 top right and bottom.
Veto S. Pascucci: 21 middle left.
Edward F. Polic: 11, 50 top, 59 bottom, 96 top, 101 top, 139 bottom.
Prince Edward Theatre: 85 top.
John Quinn: 31 top and bottom, 64 bottom.
RAF Museum: 53 top.
Denver L. Rice: 36 top left and bottom left, 37 top left, middle left and bottom left.
Connie Richards: 20 bottom left, 22 top, 23 top left, middle and bottom, 24 middle, 63 bottom left, 90 centre, 92 top left, 93 bottom left, 127 top.
Ivor Richmond: 83 all.
Harold Tienz: 54, 55 top.
Transworld Airways: 75 top right and centre.
USAF: 2/3, 44 top, 58 top, 59 bottom right, 94 top left, 123 top, 152 top.
US Naval Historical Center: 110 top, 111 top.
Robert Warren: 32 bottom.
Western Evening News (Desmond Lavers): 113 top.
John Woolnough: 18 top, 19 top left.

Contents

Glenn Miller meets some of his fans at the Hitcham air depot at Wattisham on July 24, 1944 (see page 134).

Radio Times (incorporating World-Radio) July 14 1944
Vol. 84 No. 1085 Registered at the G.P.O. as a Newspaper

A.E.F. EDITION

PROGRAMMES FOR
July 16—22

RADIO TIMES

JOURNAL OF THE BRITISH BROADCASTING CORPORATION

GLENN MILLER for your A.E.F. Programme

Sgt. JOHNNY DESMOND used to sing with Gene Krupa

GLENN MILLER, the Moonlight Serenader

DANCE-music enthusiasts in the A.E.F. will have noticed a lot of new names in their programmes since last Sunday, and among them one that is known wherever swing has a following. Glenn Miller, the Moonlight Serenader, is now broadcasting regularly in the A.E.F. Programme.

Glenn Miller has not got a 'name band' nowadays. He is a captain in the U.S. Army, and for two years he has been running a band for the Air Forces Training Command. Now he has brought his band to Britain and it has been officially designated the American Band of the Supreme Allied Command. Its primary job is to broadcast to the A.E.F., and this is the job that arouses the enthusiasm of Glenn Miller himself and every man in his band. It is a job they have all been looking forward to, and one they all thoroughly enjoy. They will make a certain number of personal appearances at benefits and in hospitals for Allied Forces, but the first charge on their time and resources will be their broadcasts to you in your programme.

Every Thursday night Glenn Miller will conduct the full band in a half-hour broadcast (20.30-21.00 DBST) in which he will introduce famous British guest artists and visiting stars. This full band numbers forty players, and they include some of the

Drummer Sgt. RAY McKINLEY, who led a famous peacetime band of his own

Sgt. MEL POWELL, formerly pianist with Benny Goodman

finest players of American dance music. For instance : Drummer Sergeant Ray McKinley, who led his own band ; Sergeant Mel Powell, formerly pianist with Benny Goodman ; Sergeant Carmen Mastren, who played guitar with Tommy Dorsey ; Sergeant Bobby Nichols, whom swing fans will remember with Vaughn Munroe. Leading vocalist is Sergeant Johnny Desmond, who used to sing with Gene Krupa. By this time, those of you who have been able to listen will have discovered for yourselves what happens when a bunch of experts like this gets together in a big band with Glenn Miller in charge. The result is a band such as nobody heard in peacetime ; it is a weekly special performance for the A.E.F.

Strings of Famous American Symphony Orchestras

Besides the big show on Thursday nights, the talent that has come over with Glenn Miller will contribute several other special programmes to the A.E.F. Programme. On Tuesday at 20.05 you will hear broadcasts conducted by Ray McKinley, with a band comparable in make-up to the pre-war Glenn Miller band. On Monday and Wednesday at 19.45 there are fifteen-minute programmes by 'Strings with Wings,' a twenty-piece string band formed from the full band, including members of America's most famous symphony orchestras, and conducted by Sergeant George Ockner, who used to be concert-master with some of America's leading radio orchestras.

Watch for them in the programmes, and for other combinations like the swing sextet with Mel Powell at the piano, the string quartet, and Johnny Desmond's own programme of songs supported by the entire band.

From *Combat Diary* at one end of the scale to Glenn Miller's musicians at the other, the A.E.F. Programme plans to bring you new broadcasts of every type specially intended for you. It is your programme. Let us know what you think of it, what you like, and what you want—the address to write to is : The Director, Allied Expeditionary Forces Programme, BBC, London, W.1. Your letters will be a great help.

One other thing : the team that Glenn Miller has brought over is called 'The American Band of the Supreme Allied Command.' It will soon be joined by the British and Canadian Bands of the Supreme Allied Command. Watch the programmes for their first broadcasts.

A.E.F. (pages 2, 4, and 20), HOME SERVICE, and GENERAL FORCES PROGRAMMES for the week

'We have been awfully busy since arriving here. During the month of August we played at 35 different bases and during our "spare time" did 44 broadcasts. It damned near killed the guys but the reaction to the band's appearances is so great that the boys eat it up despite the ruggedness. We, the band, didn't come here to set any fashions in music or to create any new swing styles — we came merely to bring a much-needed "Hunk O' Home" to some lads who have been here a couple of years. I am so firmly convinced that these boys over here ARE great that, should I have a band after the war, and should any of them desire a job, I would gladly give it to him regardless of his musical proficiencies.'

Letter from Glenn Miller, August 1944

Glenn Miller's younger brother Herb (right) with his son, John, pictured in London in 1987 shortly before Herb's death.

Foreword by John Miller

Along with my good buddy Chris Way, I've been asked many questions about just where my late uncle Glenn Miller and his band played while over in England. Wherever the Herb Miller Band and I appear, I get asked nightly by at least three or maybe four people: 'Did Glenn play here?'

Well, here at last are the answers and more. What a book and what a guy Chris Way is. He is without a doubt one of the greatest, if not the most knowledgeable, of all the Glenn Miller historians around today.

In this, his third book, he takes yet another point of view on a subject that many have never thought about. Well done good buddy, 'It's Peachy'.

John Miller
March 1996

Introduction

During the decades following World War II, the story of Major Glenn Miller and his US Army Air Force orchestra became legendary. Never before in the history of popular music had there been a dance band quite like it; that there would ever be one again was highly unlikely. Today, over 50 years later, there are those who still ardently insist that it was the greatest musical organisation of its type of all time.

In the summer of 1942, Glenn Miller, with his civilian band, was at the pinnacle of his fame and fortune. He had featured in two highly successful Hollywood motion pictures, *Sun Valley Serenade* in 1941 and *Orchestra Wives* made in the spring of 1942, and his famous Chesterfield cigarette programme was on the air three nights a week.

Back in the summer of 1941, Glenn had paid for a programme which saluted the young men who were then being drafted and were already in uniform. War clouds were quickly going to bring the United States into a full scale world war. Glenn's programme *Sunset Serenade* saluted these men in the services. Then, on a quiet peaceful Sunday in December, the Japanese attacked Pearl Harbor, bringing the USA into the front line.

In September 1942, Miller disbanded his civilian band and joined the United States Army with the rank of captain. After two months' training, Captain Glenn Miller was transferred to the Army Air Forces and given the job of forming bands. Glenn had his own ideas about modern swing music but many of these fell by the wayside in the face of the established traditions in the regular army. Nevertheless, his idea of a super band did eventually come into being.

During the spring of 1943, Captain Miller started to put together an orchestra comprising more than 40 players. Unlike his dance band, this included a large string section led by Staff Sergeant George Ockner; top flight musicians like former bandleader and drummer, Ray McKinley; pianist, arranger and composer Mel Powell from Benny Goodman's Dance Band; trumpeter Bernie Priven; clarinet player Michael 'Peanuts' Hucko, and many other top musicians from all the leading swing bands. Also included in the line-up were singers Tony Martin, Bob Huston and a 'Glee Club' singing group. Several old Miller players re-joined their former boss: bass player Herman 'Trigger' Alpert; arranger Jerry Gray, and Glenn's band manager, Donald Haynes.

This particular concert took place in the Drill Hall of the US Naval Construction Training Center at Camp Endicott, Davisville, Rhode Island. The most well-known photograph of the man himself is this one taken in 1943 in the RCA Victor Studios in New York City by the De Bellis studio.

Born in Clarinda, Iowa, on March 1, 1904, Glenn's early years were marked with the struggle to survive and the spectre of financial ruin. After many false starts, he obtained his first big break when his band was booked to play at the Glen Island Casino at New Rochelle in New York State on May 17, 1939.

The performance was being broadcast and the distinctive blend between reeds, clarinet and saxophones caused a sensation. As drummer Moe Purtill recalled: 'It was a phenomenon'. Here, Glenn plays his chosen instrument during a recording session in 1939 at the RCA Victor Studios in New York City.

On May 29, 1943, the orchestra broadcast the first of six local test programmes over the CBS network in a series called *I Sustain the Wings*, the name taken from the motto of the Army Air Forces, *Sustineo Alas*. Then, on July 17, Glenn and his Army Air Forces Training Command Orchestra, as it was known, made their first coast to coast broadcast. Needless to say it was an outstanding success from the moment the green light for airtime came on.

For nearly a year, Glenn broadcast every Saturday and the programme brought in many millions of dollars for the war effort. The orchestra also played at War Bond rallies and at 'WAC' (Women's Army Auxiliary Corps) recruiting drives throughout the eastern states of America during the first half of 1944.

During the build-up for the invasion of Europe, Colonel Edward Kirby, who was in charge of the radio network that was to begin broadcasting once the invasion had begun, to be called the Allied Expeditionary Forces Programme (AEFP), was sent to Washington D.C. and New York City to obtain equipment. Kirby had also been given the task of obtaining an American radio orchestra to broadcast to the Allied forces from London. Kirby, who was based at the Supreme Headquarters of the Allied Expeditionary Force (SHAEF) at Bushy Park, near Teddington, Middlesex, thought that the best person to ask about an orchestra would be Captain Glenn Miller. 'What about my orchestra?' replied Glenn, and as soon as Kirby got back to London, he went straight to see General Eisenhower's naval aide, Commander Harry Butcher, who loved the idea.

On June 18, Miller and his radio producer, Technical Sergeant Paul Dudley, flew to England while the orchestra,

comprising some 60 members, and now known as the American Band of the Supreme Allied Command, left New York aboard the liner *Queen Elizabeth*. After being chased by a pack of U-Boats in mid-Atlantic, they disembarked at Gourock on the Firth of Clyde in Scotland, in the early hours of June 28. Miller and Dudley, who had already arrived at Renfrew on June 21 and had spent the next few days in London on advance preparations, were there to meet the band at Gourock. The whole party then travelled by overnight troop train to London.

London was not a safe place to be in during late June 1944. Since the 13th, one week after D-Day, it had been under constant attack by V1 flying bombs and, no sooner had the train pulled in to Euston station, than an alert was sounded. Miller's musicians were due to be billeted at Sloane Court in Chelsea, an area already nicknamed 'Buzz-Bomb Alley', because of the number of flying bombs passing over the area. Consequently, Miller, and his Executive Officer and band manager, 2nd Lieutenant Don Haynes, went straight out to SHAEF at Bushy Park to arrange to transfer the band to a safer location. They saw Colonel Kirby in his position of US Director of Troop Broadcasting, and his deputy, Lieutenant-Colonel David Niven, the British film star, who suggested Bedford, and all four visited the town to inspect the facilities that very afternoon.

The band was transferred to Bedford on Sunday, July 2; the next morning, their former billet was hit by a V1. During the coming week, they turned the building known as Co-Partners Hall (used by the Social Club for the Bedford Gas Works) into a small radio studio and settled into their new billets in Ashburnham Road.

By September 1942, with two feature films behind him (see page 146), Glenn Miller had become a household name but that month he dissolved his band and joined the US Army. However, it was not until the following year that his talents were acknowledged within the service and he was allowed to form his own orchestra to entertain the troops. His American Band of the Supreme Allied Command arrived in Britain in June 1944, their first 'base' concert taking place on July 14 at Thurleigh. Airfield concerts comprised a little under a third of the band's performances, the onset of the British winter putting paid to any more appearances in draughty, cold hangars after the Kingscliffe concert on October 3. Although the airbases chosen were invariably American (the RAF had their own performances by the Squadronaires), there seems to be no rhyme or reason as to their selection. Here, Glenn meets Colonel Hubert Zemke, the CO of the 56th Fighter Group, during the Boxted concert on August 6.

On the evening of Sunday, July 9, the band made its first radio broadcast over the AEF programme network, AFN (American Forces Network) and the BBC Home Service; it was an outstanding success. Subsequently, several smaller units from within the orchestra played over the AEF: the string section broadcast on their own in a programme called *Strings With Wings*; the dance band, under Sergeant Ray McKinley, broadcast a show called *The Swing Shift*, while Sergeant Mel Powell led a small swing sextet in a programme called *The Uptown Hall*. Singer Sergeant Johnny Desmond (who had replaced Tony Martin back in October 1943 in the USA) had his own show called *Sergeant Johnny Desmond Sings* (for which the entire orchestra were directed by arranger Sergeant Norman Leyden). The relief pianist, Jack Russin, also had his own programme called *Piano Parade* on Saturday mornings.

Once a week, the entire 'gang', as Glenn called them, got together on Thursday evenings, with either a visiting British or American guest star, to produce a half-hour programme called *The American Band of the Supreme Allied Command*.

On the afternoon of Friday, July 14, Miller and a 40-piece orchestra gave their first base concert at Thurleigh airfield, near Bedford. It was an outstanding success. The roar that went up from the GIs packed into the large B-17 hangar, made Glenn remark to Colonel Kirby in the interval: 'Making all the money in the band business could never make me feel this rich!' Many more concerts followed throughout the British Isles during the summer of 1944.

On August 1, at the insistence of General Eisenhower, all the three AEF orchestras: the American (Glenn's); the British, under RSM George Melachrino; and the Canadian (later directed by Captain Robert Farnon) were renamed respectively the American Band of the AEF, the British Band of the AEF and the Canadian Band of the AEF.

Glenn's first base concert using the new title took place on Wednesday, August 2, at Kimbolton airfield.

The radio schedule continued unchanged throughout the summer and early autumn (fall) of 1944. The airfield and field hospital concerts continued until October 3 by which time the weather and darker nights curtailed further performances. The last few had caused many problems. Airfield hangars were cold and the doors were usually left open and, at several of the later concerts, Glenn and the band had to perform wearing gloves, overcoats and woollen underwear. Wearing gloves to play was very difficult, particularly for the strings, and George Ockner performed no mean task when he played *The Flight of the Bumble Bee* on a violin whilst wearing gloves which says much for his musicianship.

Due to the cancelled airfield concerts, Glenn, who had been promoted to the rank of major on August 17, was able to expand the radio broadcasts over the AEF programme. During mid-November, the radio schedule was further increased and the full 40-piece orchestra made two half-hour

broadcasts every week. Nearly all of these were performed in front of an audience of some 2,500 service personnel at the Queensbury All Services Club in Old Compton Street, London.

Then, after a trip to Paris in late November, Glenn informed all the 62 members of his orchestra that they would be leaving for a six-week stay in the French capital over Christmas. He also said 'that they would be playing for 30,000 to 40,000 GIs of the fighting forces of the AEF, giving them a "Hunk 'O Home".'

At Steeple Morden on August 18, Sergeant Johnny Desmond gives a solo vocal during the afternoon concert attended by a reported 5,000 officers and men of the 355th Fighter Group joined by others from the 91st Bomb Group based at nearby Bassingbourn. (Contrary to local legend, the latter base never had a Miller concert of its own.) In an interview with Vernon Harris of the BBC on September 14, Glenn claimed that 'in the month of August, we played 89 separate jobs. That includes 35 concerts at the bases and camps, as well as maintaining our regular broadcasting schedule.'

Glenn sent his second in command, Don Haynes, ahead to Paris on Saturday, November 25, where he met their old friend from the Bedfordshire headquarters of the VIII Service Command at Milton Ernest, Lieutenant Colonel Norman F. Baessell. During the time that Haynes was away, Glenn and the band spent their time in Bedford recording a stockpile of broadcasts. Lieutenant Haynes returned on Saturday, December 2, and by the 12th, the orchestra, working day and night, had recorded all the programmes to be broadcast during their stay in Paris.

On Tuesday evening, December 12, 1944, Major Glenn Miller and the American Band of the AEF gave their last live broadcast at the Queensbury Club. The guest that evening was the Irish-American singer, Morton Downey. The weather was terrible with thick fog blanketing much of western Europe. Don Haynes was scheduled to depart for France the following day, to prepare for their arrival, and to make sure that there would be transport awaiting in Paris when Glenn

and the rest of the band arrived. However, Miller was far from happy with this arrangement and told Haynes in no uncertain terms to change the orders so that he could personally precede the band on or about December 14.

However, on that Thursday, Glenn was still fog-bound in London so Colonel Baessell offered to give Glenn a lift to Paris the next day. At 1.55 p.m. on Friday, December 15, Miller and Baessell took off from RAF Twinwood Farm in a single-engined Norseman piloted by Flight Officer Johnny 'Nipper' Morgan. They were never seen again. Three days later, the American Band of the AEF flew to Paris, to discover not only no transport but, more importantly, no commanding officer.

The orchestra remained on the Continent of Europe for the next seven and a half months; in fact, they never did return to England. They toured and gave concerts in every part of France, Germany and Holland and returned to the USA in August 1945, before being disbanded in late November.

Glenn Miller was posthumously awarded the Bronze Star for his service in the ETO, which was presented to his widow on **March 23, 1945. Here, Helen is pictured with Colonel F. R. Kerr in the office of David Mackay (the Millers' lawyer) in New York.**

It was only to be expected that 50 years on from Glenn Miller's wartime tour of Britain, anniversary concerts would be organised but, of all the venues at which his music was played in 1994, to Miller fans, Twinwood Farm airfield must remain closest to the heart. Being the nearest to Bedford, not only was this RAF airfield frequently used when the band returned from a concert, but it was also the scene of the final tragedy when Glenn took off from here for France. By way of extending a thank you, the band had given the station personnel their own special concert on August 27, 1944 — the only one they held specifically for the RAF. *Above:* Fifty years later (all but a day), the Glenn Miller (UK) Orchestra, one of the two bands which officially carry the Miller flame today, gave a very special anniversary concert. *Below:* In the background of this shot can be seen the derelict control tower, in front of which Glenn waited for the arrival of the aircraft which was to carry him to his death.

After the 50th anniversary events in 1994, the success of the Anglia television programme *Moonlight Serenade — Glenn Miller in England,* and the extremely popular display on Glenn Miller at the Imperial War Museum at Duxford, all of which I was involved in, I came up with the idea of this book.

It lists and illustrates every location that Glenn Miller and his orchestra stayed at and performed at during their stay in the British Isles. It gives Glenn Miller fans a closer insight into many of the wartime locations and areas that have never been covered before, and also goes one step further by bringing them to life over 50 years later through the comparison 'then and now' photographs. It is also a trip down memory lane for those who lived through 1944 and perhaps saw the band in action.

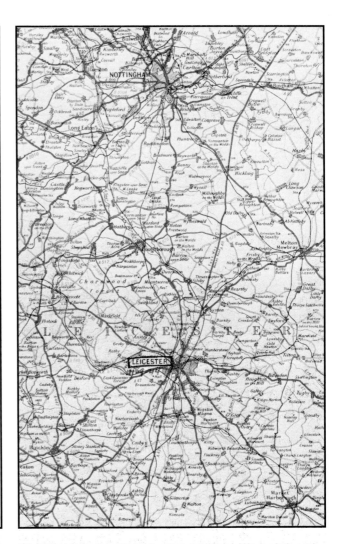

Date	Location	Type	Page
14-7-44	THURLEIGH - MOTOR TRANSPORT		PAGE 60
16-7-44	MILTON ERNEST - "	"	60
28-7-44	MELCHBOURNE PARK "	"	60
29-7-44	WATTISHAM-HITCHAM "	"	62
25-7-44	NEWBURY	AIR TRANSPORT - "	76
28-7-44	POLEBROOK	MOTOR TRANSPORT	60
29-7-44	PINETREE	" "	70
31-7-44	ABBOTTS-RIPTON	" "	60
2-8-44	KIMBOLTON	" "	60
4-8-44	"FORWARD"	AIR TRANSPORT	79
6-8-44	BOXTED	AIR TRANSPORT	62
6-8-44	HALESWORTH	" "	63
7-8-44	CIRENCESTER	" "	69
9-8-44	SHAEF	MOTOR TRANSPORT	71
12-8-44	GROVE	AIR TRANSPORT	69
13-8-44	LANGFORDLODGE, IRELAND	"	
14-8-44	WARTON	AIR TRANSPORT	30
			38
15-8-44	BURTONWOOD "	"	
16-8-44	BENTLEY-PRIORY	" + MOTOR "	71
18-8-44	STEEPLE-MORDEN	AIR TRANSPORT	61
18-8-44	ATTLEBRIDGE	" "	53
23-8-44	PODINGTON	MOTOR TRANSPORT	60
23-8-44	FRAMLINGHAM	AIR TRANSPORT	63
25-8-44	KNETTISHALL	"	62
25-8-44	WENDLING	"	53
27-8-44	TWINWOOD FARMS	MOTOR "	60
28-8-44	PLYMOUTH	AIR TRANSPORT	88
1-9-44	TIBENHAM	"	63
10-9-44	HORHAM	"	63
11-9-44	LEICESTER	MOTOR "	49
12-9-44	HARDWICKE	AIR "	63
15-9-44	RUFFAM	MOTOR "	62
24-9-44	N. WITHAM	"	50
24-9-44	GRANTHAM	"	50
1-10-44	ELMSWELL	"	62
2-10-44	NUTHAMPSTEAD	"	50
			61
3-10-44	KINGS CLIFFE	"	50

During his stay in England, Glenn used a Geographers' Atlas to mark the location of various bases where concerts were given. On the flyleaf *(left)*, he made up a simple index in date order. After the war, the atlas was donated by the Miller family to the US Air Force Museum and it is now on display at Dayton, Ohio.

(Unfortunately the flyleaf is now missing.) We had the atlas photographed specially for this book and have included reproductions of every page on which Glenn has made annotations. Some places are marked yet no concert was performed; we can only speculate as to the reason why.

I considered the two basic ways of presenting Glenn's British concerts: either chronologically or alphabetically by location. Both methods have advantages and disadvantages, but in the end I decided that readers would most probably prefer to read about each venue separately rather than dodge around the country in the date order of each performance. The locations are therefore presented alphabetically, but I have included a chronological listing for those who wish to consult Glenn's daily schedule during the period he spent in the United Kingdom from July to December 1944.

Over the years, Glenn Miller is rumoured to have played in many locations which he never visited, like the so-called Dorset concerts in September 1944. The fact is that these concerts were given by the US Navy Dance Band, led by Sam Donahue, which was also in England at the same time as Miller's American Band of the AEF.

Every aspect has been used or taken into account in the preparation of this book. Newspaper archives and photo archives have been checked, and local people have given details of several previously unknown concerts. Three important members of the band kept diaries which have been cross-checked against the atlas that Glenn himself kept of the locations where they performed. I also tapped into the joint photographic collections held by myself and good friends, Edward F. Polic and Richard C. March, which comprise the three largest AEF band photo collections in the world. Between us we own over 700-plus photographs of the orchestra in Europe.

So the outcome is this book. Happy reading!

Chris Way, December 1995

December 1994: Author Chris Way reflects on the events of 50 years before in the control tower at Twinwood Farm.

Melchbourne Park — an VIII Air Force Service Command ordnance depot in Bedfordshire — the venue on July 21, 1944

GLENN MILLER'S ACTIVITIES IN GREAT BRITAIN DURING 1944

July 8
Milton Ernest Hall — Ray McKinley Quartet

July 9
Corn Exchange, Bedford — American Band of the SAC

July 13
Corn Exchange, Bedford — American Band of the SAC

July 14
Thurleigh airfield — GM & American Band of the SAC

July 16
Milton Ernest Hall — GM & American Band of the SAC

July 20
Corn Exchange, Bedford — GM & American Band of the SAC

July 21
Melchbourne Park — GM & American Band of the SAC

July 23
American Red Cross Club, Bromham Road, Bedford — String Orchestra

July 24
Wattisham airfield — GM & Dance Band

July 25
Greenham Common airfield — GM & American Band of the SAC
Newbury Corn Exchange — GM & American Band of the SAC

July 27
American Red Cross Club, Rainbow Corner — Ray McKinley & Dance Band
Plaza Cinema, Piccadilly — GM & American Band of the SAC

July 28
Polebrook airfield — GM & American Band of the SAC

July 29
Wycombe Abbey HQ, High Wycombe — GM & American Band of the SAC

July 30
Queensbury All Services Club — GM & American Band of the SAC

July 31
Abbots Ripton/Alconbury — Ray McKinley & Dance Band

August 1
Milton Ernest Hall — Small Dance Band

August 2
Kimbolton airfield — GM & Dance Band

August 3
Co-Partners Hall, Bedford — GM & AEF Orchestra

August 4
Southwick House, Portsmouth — GM & AEF Orchestra

August 5
Milton Ernest Hall — Small Dance Band

August 6
Milton Ernest — String Orchestra
Halesworth airfield — GM & Dance Band
Boxted airfield — GM & Dance Band

August 7
US Army General Hospital, Cirencester — GM & Dance Band

August 9
SHAEF Bushy Park — GM & AEF Orchestra

August 10
American Red Cross Club, Rainbow Corner — Ray McKinley & Dance Band
Paris Cinema, London — GM & AEF Orchestra

August 11
Corn Exchange, Bedford — GM & AEF Orchestra
Milton Ernest Hall — Small Dance Band

August 12
Grove airfield — Mel Powell Small Dance Band

August 13
American Red Cross Club, Belfast — GM & Dance Band
Langford Lodge airfield — GM & Dance Band

August 14
Warton airfield — GM & Dance Band

August 15
Burtonwood airfield — GM & Dance Band

August 16
RAF Hendon airfield — In Transit
RAF Bentley Priory — GM & AEF Orchestra

August 18
Steeple Morden airfield — GM & AEF Orchestra
Attlebridge airfield — GM & AEF Orchestra
Samson & Hercules Ballroom, Norwich — GM & Dance Band

August 20
Boxted airfield — Mel Powell & Small Band

August 23
Podington airfield — GM & AEF Orchestra
Framlingham airfield — GM & AEF Orchestra

August 25
Wendling airfield — GM & AEF Orchestra
Knettishall airfield — GM & AEF Orchestra

August 26
Steeple Morden airfield — Small Dance Band

August 27
Twinwood Farm airfield — GM & AEF Orchestra
Queensbury All Services Club — Bing Crosby

August 28 (Plymouth, Devon)
Manadon Field Hospital — GM & Dance Band
HMS Drake Seabee Base — String Orchestra
Shapter's Field — GM & Dance Band
Manadon Field Hospital — String Orchestra
Odeon Cinema, Plymouth — GM & AEF Orchestra

August 29
Hardwick airfield — Concert cancelled
Wormingford airfield — Concert cancelled

August 30
Kettner's Restaurant, London — Bing Crosby sings to crowd

August 31
American Red Cross Club,
   Rainbow Corner, London — Ray McKinley & Dance Band
Paris Cinema, London — GM & AEF Orchestra
Stage Door Canteen, London — Bing Crosby

September 1
Tibenham airfield — GM & Dance Band
Thorpe Abbotts airfield — GM & Dance Band

September 2
Queensbury All Services Club — GM & AEF Orchestra

September 3
Feldman Swing Club, London — Quartet

September 7
American Red Cross Club,
   Goldington Road, Bedford — Small Dance Band

September 8
Thurleigh airfield — Swing Sextet

September 10
Horham airfield — GM & AEF Orchestra

September 11
De Montfort Hall, Leicester — GM & AEF Orchestra

September 12
Wormingford airfield — GM & AEF Orchestra
Hardwick airfield — GM & AEF Orchestra

September 14
American Red Cross Club,
   Rainbow Corner, London — Ray McKinley & Dance Band
Queensbury All Services Club — GM & AEF Orchestra

September 15
Bury St Edmunds airfield — Ray McKinley & AEF Orchestra

September 16
Abbey Road Studios, London — GM & AEF Orchestra

September 17
Feldman Swing Club, London — Small Jazz Group

September 21
Queensbury All Services Club — GM & AEF Orchestra

September 22
American Red Cross Club,
   Midland Road, Bedford — Small Dance Band

September 24
North Witham airfield — GM & AEF Orchestra
State Theatre, Grantham — GM & AEF Orchestra

September 25
US 91st General Hospital,
   Oxford — GM & AEF Orchestra
Mount Farm airfield — GM & AEF Orchestra

September 28
American Red Cross Club,
   Rainbow Corner, London — Ray McKinley & Dance Band
Queensbury All Services Club — GM & AEF Orchestra

October 1
Great Ashfield airfield — Ray McKinley & AEF Orchestra

October 2
Nuthampstead airfield — Ray McKinley & AEF Orchestra

October 3
Kingscliffe airfield — GM & AEF Orchestra

October 5
Queensbury All Services Club — GM & AEF Orchestra

October 12
Queensbury All Services Club — GM & AEF Orchestra

October 15
Stoll Theatre, London — GM & AEF Orchestra
Feldman Swing Club, London — Mel Powell & Michael Hucko

October 19
Queensbury All Services Club — GM & AEF Orchestra

October 26
Queensbury All Services Club — GM & AEF Orchestra

October 29
American Red Cross Club,
   Midland Road, Bedford — Small Dance Band

October 30
Abbey Road Studios, London — GM & AEF Orchestra

November 2
Queensbury All Services Club — GM & AEF Orchestra
Kettner's Restaurant, London — Dinner in honour of GM & AEF Orchestra

November 6
Abbey Road Studios, London — GM & AEF Orchestra
BBC Maida Vale Studio,
   London — String Orchestra

November 9
Queensbury All Services Club — GM & AEF Orchestra

November 11
Milton Ernest Hall — Swing Sextet

November 13
Abbey Road Studios, London — GM & AEF Orchestra
BBC Maida Vale Studio,
   London — AEF Orchestra

November 14
Queensbury All Services Club — AEF Orchestra

November 17
Queensbury All Services Club — AEF Orchestra

November 20
Abbey Road Studios, London — GM & AEF Orchestra

November 21
Queensbury All Services Club — GM & AEF Orchestra

November 23
Milton Ernest Hall — Ray McKinley & Swing Shift

November 24
Queensbury All Services Club — GM & AEF Orchestra

November 26
Granada Cinema, Bedford — Glenn Miller — Judge

November 27
Abbey Road Studios, London — GM & AEF Orchestra

November 28
Queensbury All Services Club — GM & AEF Orchestra

December 5
Queensbury All Services Club — GM & AEF Orchestra

December 6
Abbey Road Studios, London — Christmas messages recorded by Glenn Miller, Don Haynes and Paul Dudley

December 12
Queensbury All Services Club — GM & AEF Orchestra
Kettner's Restaurant — Farewell party
Mount Royal Hotel, London — GM awaits flight to Paris

December 13
Mount Royal Hotel, London — GM awaits flight to Paris

December 15
RAF Twinwood Farm — Final flight

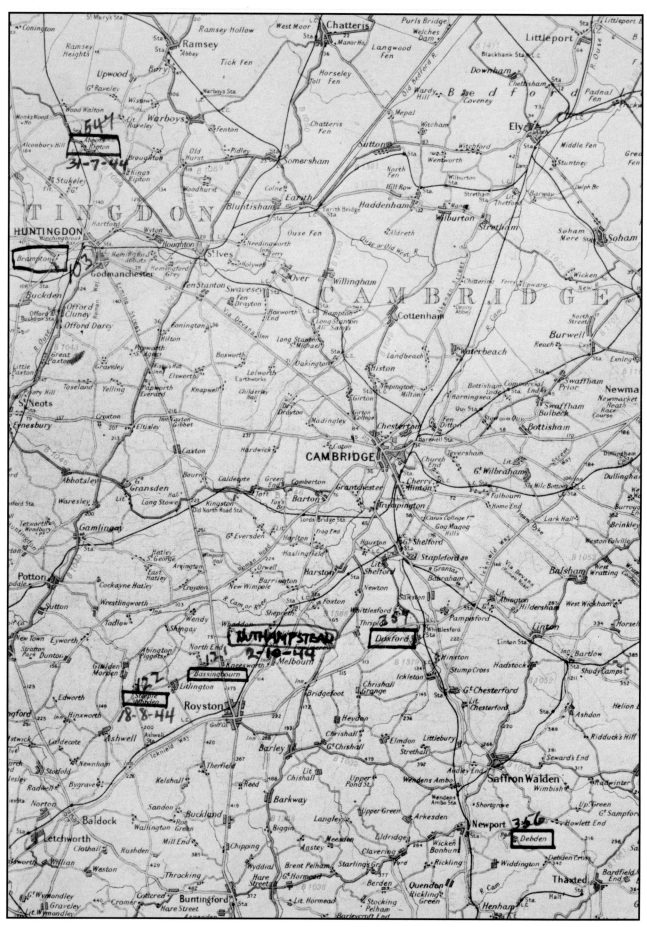

The hand of Glenn Miller on the face of England. His annotations on this page of his Geographers' Atlas include Abbots Ripton, location of the July 31 concert. However, as we can see from this and other pages, Glenn also marked bases (by their US station number) where no concert was performed, viz: Bassingbourn, Brampton, Debden and Duxford. Possibly, they were venues which never materialised or merely to show which nearby bases might send personnel to attend.

Abbots Ripton Station 547

HUNTINGDONSHIRE

The 2nd Strategic Air Depot at Abbots Ripton, Huntingdonshire (now part of Cambridgeshire), shared the base of the 482nd Bomb Group at Alconbury (Station 102). The SAD at Abbots Ripton came under the jurisdiction of the VIII Air Force Service Command headquarters located at Milton Ernest Hall at Milton Ernest, just to the north of Bedford.

On Monday, July 31, 1944, during the evening, the 19-piece dance band section of Captain Glenn Miller's American Band of the Supreme Allied Command, with vocalists under the direction of drummer Technical Sergeant Ray McKinley, performed in one of the supply hangars to some 5,000 personnel,

Often seen in contemporary documents spelt 'Abbotts Ripton' with two 't's, the 2nd Strategic Air Depot lay on the south-eastern side of the airfield at Alconbury. It is also sometimes referred to as a separate airfield in its own right but it shared the same field with the 482nd Bomb Group although both units had a different station number. Alconbury continued as a USAF base after the war; in fact until 1995 it was the only Eighth Air Force station to have been in continuous use by US forces since World War II, the air depot site extensively altered and partially devoted to housing being still referred to as Abbots Ripton. The closure of Alconbury was announced by the Pentagon in May 1993 and its aircraft withdrawn two years later. By comparing the 1995 aerial photo, (above) with the 1945 plan (right) the surviving buildings can be identified, but unfortunately, it has not been possible to establish just which of the six large assembly hangars was used for the July 31 performance.

many of them from the 482nd. After dinner at the depot, the band returned by road transport to their base in Bedford.

Abbots Ripton would feature again in December 1944 as Glenn Miller's pilot on his final, fatal flight, Flight Officer John R. S. 'Nipper' Morgan, took off from there on December 15. (The circumstances surrounding Glenn's disappearance are described on page 136.)

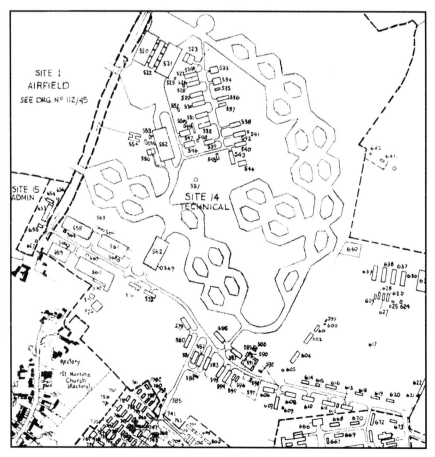

Attlebridge, Station 120

NORFOLK

On the afternoon of Friday, August 18, a flight of B-24 Liberators, including a red and white zig-zag lead ship from the 466th Bomb Group at Attlebridge, collected Major Glenn Miller (he was promoted on August 17) and the entire American Band of the AEF (renamed on August 1) from the RAF airfield of Twinwood Farm just north of Bedford and flew them to the 355th Fighter Group base at Steeple Morden near Royston, Cambridgeshire. There, Glenn and the orchestra gave a concert for the 355th and members of the 91st Bomb Group from the nearby bomber base at Bassingbourn. After the performance at Steeple Morden, the band loaded their instruments, music stands, etc., on board the B-24s which flew back to their home base of Attlebridge which had been taken over by the 466th in 1943.

The airfield lies eight miles north-west of Norwich near the village of Weston Longville and, between 8 and 9 p.m., Glenn and the band, along with special guests Rudy Starita's All Girl Orchestra and Hollywood film star Colonel James Stewart, performed in the northern hangar. Among the numbers played was *In the Mood* and many other hits. This concert was a 100-mission party for officers and enlisted personnel and was attended by 10,000 from this base and others in the area.

The band was accommodated overnight at Attlebridge and returned the next morning by road transport to Bedford where their billets were located.

Major Glenn Miller and Sergeant Jimmy Priddy perform for the 466th Bomb Group on the evening of August 18. Earlier that Friday, the group had been on an operation to Woippy in north-eastern France but the actual 100th mission by the 466th had taken place ten days earlier to Chartres, west of Paris.

Unusually, the band performed in the northernmost hangar on the far side of the airfield — possibly it was too difficult to clear the one on the technical site. The latter is now part of the Bernard Matthews turkey empire but the site of the northern T2, dismantled around 1950, is now owned by a local farmer, John Hurst. Most of the concrete base has been removed save for a strip along the eastern entrance, fortuitously providing the link with its musical and military past.

When the concert had finished, Glenn retired to the Officers' Mess where one of the pilots, Captain John Woolnough, asked Miller, who was then in conversation with the station chaplain, Fred A. Walker, if he could have his photograph taken with him to send to his brother who was a great fan of the band. Miller agreed provided the picture could be taken somewhere out of the limelight to avoid more requests for photos, but the only room which could be found unlocked was the toilet! Miller is reported to have been much amused; this is the unique picture of Miller and Woolnough taken by Sergeant Russell Clements that Friday evening. Today, although the Officers' Mess on Site No. 2, east of Paddy's Lane, has gone, the Editor and his wife managed to locate the spot in the woodland which now covers the mouldering foundations.

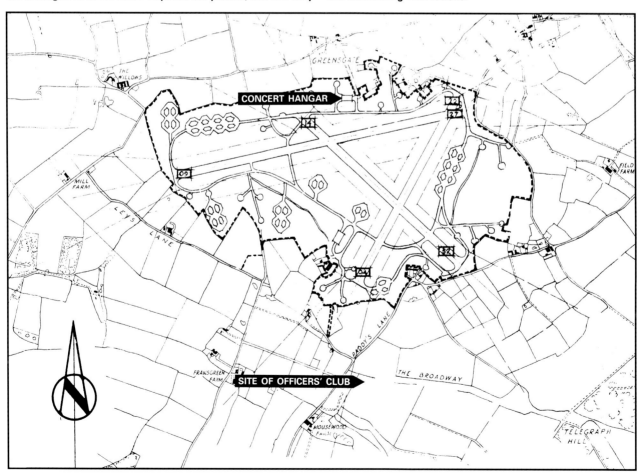

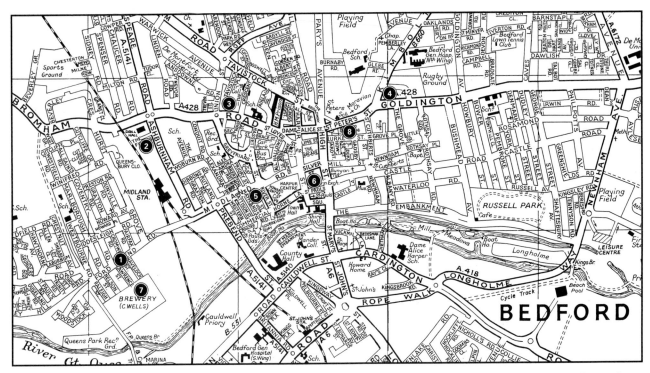

Bedford

The county town of Bedford, some 50-odd miles north of London, was an ideal base for the Glenn Miller band as it was close to East Anglia and the many United States Army Air Force bomber and fighter stations. It also had direct lines into the BBC's Broadcasting House in London, and was already the home of the BBC Symphony Orchestra under Sir Adrian Boult. Facilities were also available to accommodate Glenn's large orchestra.

Miller first visited the town on Thursday, June 29 with his second-in-command, 2nd Lieutenant Don Haynes, and Lieutenant-Colonel David Niven, British film star turned liaison officer, to view possible billets and broadcasting studios in the town. The orchestra members were moved from their short-term billets in Sloane Court, London, on the morning of Sunday, July 2.

As will become clear, Bedford came to play an important part in the last chapter of Glenn Miller's life, having many connections with his six-month stay in the British Isles which are still evident to this day. Glenn loved the idea of eating fish and chips from newspaper and, although no wartime photograph exists of him so doing, the shop in question still stands today, although sadly no longer a fish and chip shop. Now it is an

Indian take-away, on the corner of Lawrence Street. Other buildings, too, can still be found around the town that played host to the legendary Miller band, a walking tour of all the sites taking about 90 minutes.

Glenn Miller's fish and chip shop, [1] on the plan, has since adopted eastern cuisine. At the far end of Lawrence Street stands Co-Partners Hall, used by the band for rehearsals and broadcasts.

Left: American Eighth Army Air Force officers of the 1st Air Division parade round St Paul's Square, Bedford, to receive the freedom of the city. Although the men have marched into the pages of history, the present day view *(right)* is remarkably similar, with the gateway to the churchyard on the left and Magistrates Court in the background.

20

American Red Cross billets [2] in Ashburnham Road were allocated to the band for their quarters in Bedford. No. 42 is on the left with Bishopstone House on the right. Currently both buildings are boarded up, the car park being used by visitors to the new government and local council offices which have been erected at their rear.

Ashburnham Road

BEDFORD

No. 42-44 Ashburnham Road was the main billet for the entire 60 enlisted men from Glenn Miller's American Band of the AEF during their six-month stay in England. Ashburnham Road was used as an annexe to the American Red Cross Club in Bedford.

Major Glenn Miller with Pfc Vito Pascucci, the orchestra's instrument repair man, outside Bishopstone House during the summer of 1944.

Orchestra saxophone players, Staff Sergeant Hank Freeman, left, and Sergeant Vince Carbone, right, with an unidentified American Red Cross officer outside their billets.

The American Red Cross Club [3] in Bromham Road in July 1944.

The Queen outside the Club on Sunday, July 23.

Victoria Terrace in Bromham Road, Bedford. In 1934, the central part (Nos. 17-23) became a garage, seen here in 1957 just before it was extended. During the war, the showroom was converted into the American Red Cross Enlisted Men's Club.

American Red Cross Enlisted Men's Club

BROMHAM ROAD, BEDFORD

Formerly Morris House, later Kenning's Garage, the American Red Cross Enlisted Men's Club, located on the corner of Union Street and Bromham Road, often acted as home base for some of Glenn Miller's band, and small groups from within the large orchestra often played there. After the arrival of US forces in Bedford in March 1943, the garage was taken over by the American Red Cross and used as an Enlisted Men's Club until the end of the war. On Sunday, July 23, 1944, HRH Queen Elizabeth (now the Queen Mother) visited the club as part of her royal visit to Bedford. The string section from the band played for her on this occasion.

In the late 1950s, the whole terrace was taken over by the garage but this was demolished some 30 years later and has now been redeveloped with the erection of a block of residential flats.

The collection of huts which formed the basis for the American Red Cross Officers' Club [4] in Bedford has long been demolished but the building in the background still survives virtually unchanged as a combined doctor's surgery and accountant's office.

American Red Cross Officers' Club

GOLDINGTON ROAD, BEDFORD

The American Red Cross Officers' Club, on the corner of Goldington Road and Kimbolton Road, was one of several Red Cross Clubs run by Mrs Anona Moser and was used by Glenn Miller and Don Haynes for their quarters in Bedford from July to December 1944. This was the club where Haynes, who acted as the band's business manager, was introduced to the Queen on Sunday, July 23, during the royal visit to the American Red Cross in the town.

American officers and invited lady guests take to the dance floor during the small dance band's performance at the Officers' Club on September 7, 1944. Typically, the composition of this ensemble would be a small four to nine-piece group of relief musicians, headed by either Phil Cogliano or Zeke Zarchy.

Her Majesty Queen Elizabeth outside the Goldington Road Club on the afternoon of Sunday, July 23 during her tour of the American Red Cross operation in Bedford in which her sister-in-law, Lady Bowes-Lyon, gave helpful assistance.

The interior of the American Red Cross Club in Goldington Road is seen here on August 3, 1944. Mrs Anona Moser, standing at the back, was the programme director for all the Red Cross Clubs in the Bedford area.

Then and now. The first and second floors (US second and third) of Longhurst & Skinner's furniture store [5] on the corner of Midland Road and River Street were taken over for the American Red Cross Club in Bedford.

American Red Cross Club

MIDLAND ROAD, BEDFORD

The American Red Cross Club, located on the corner of Midland Road and River Street, gave additional social breathing space for American servicemen in Bedford. Small sections from within the band often played at this venue. The first occasion was on Friday, September 22, and another small concert and dance took place on Sunday, October 29.

Right: **A Christmas party on the first floor just before Christmas, 1944.**

Unfortunately, the stairs from which the 1944 picture was taken have now been enclosed under fire regulations, thus preventing an exact comparison, but today the first floor is partially devoted to a coffee shop; a unique feature which enables visitors to Bedford 50 years later to still eat and drink in an original American Red Cross Club!

'Captain Miller conducts the American Band of the Supreme Allied Command.' The very first broadcast by Glenn and the orchestra after their arrival in Great Britain was that given on July 9 from the Corn Exchange [6] in Bedford (above). Note the microphone strung on wires from the ceiling. So hurried had been the move south after their June 28 arrival at Gourock on the Clyde, that many of the band's smaller items of equipment had not yet caught up with them, as seen in this picture (right) of the trumpet section improvising with empty food tins with tape wrapped around the ends as mutes! Bottom: At some stage during the evening, Leslie Mitchell, Glenn Miller, Dorothy Carless and Bruce Trent were photographed grouped together around the microphone.

The Corn Exchange

BEDFORD

Studio No. 1, within the Corn Exchange in St Paul's Square, Bedford, was the major broadcasting venue for both Glenn Miller's band and the BBC Symphony Orchestra directed by Sir Adrian Boult. The studio was used for all the early major broadcasts by Miller and his band, the first being on Sunday, July 9. Most of the concerts and broadcasts were open to the public and the auditorium was invariably filled to overflowing with service personnel from nearby bases and camps as they took advantage of the open nature of the performances.

Glenn and the band nicknamed the Corn Exchange 'the Lambardo Hall' after Guy Lambardo, the famous American bandleader. British guest stars who performed with the band during July 1944 read like a who's who of the greatest artistes of the day: Dorothy Careless, Bruce Trent, Sergeant Jimmy Miller, Vera Lynn and Anne Shelton. Well-known announcers from the BBC included Jean Metcalfe, Captain Franklin Englemann, Leslie Mitchell, Lieutenant-Colonel David Niven and Sergeant Broderick Crawford (of post-war *Highway Patrol* fame).

The building was refurbished in the autumn of 1995, one of the first concerts in the re-opened auditorium being the special Glenn Miller Tribute Concert by the BBC Big Band on November 23 launching Bedford's Glenn Miller Festival.

Fifty years on, the Corn Exchange is still a famous venue for concerts and broadcasts. Little has changed since the first performance by the band set the scene on that summer Sunday evening when the famous Miller sound was introduced live to the British public. Four days later, on Thursday, July 13, the band and guest stars were back for a repeat performance.

On Thursday, July 20, a live BBC broadcast from the Corn Exchange featured Sergeant Jimmy Miller (leader of the RAF Squadronaires) and the British forces sweetheart, Vera Lynn. Jimmy sang the Frank Sinatra song, *This is a Lovely Way to Spend an Evening*, while Vera sang *Besame Mucho*. It was one of those lasting memories for all those present and Jimmy Miller still remembers the event well:

'As soon as Glenn Miller walked into the Corn Exchange, the whole mood of the orchestra members changed; everyone looked up; talking and laughing stopped! Compared to the Miller band, the Squadronaires were a rabble, but that is the only way to run an orchestra. Even without that lush romantic sound, the band was like a military machine. Miller asked without a word and that orchestra gave. Sorry to say my vocal was the best I could give.'

Captain Glenn Miller and the American Band of the AEF also gave an extra-special concert in order to raise money for the Lord Mayor of Bedford's Christmas Fund at the Corn Exchange on the evening of Friday, August 11.

Captain Miller introduces the band during the broadcast from the Corn Exchange which took place on the evening of Thursday, July 13, 1944.

A close colleague of Miller in England was the British film star, David Niven, then a Lieutenant-Colonel in the Rifle Brigade. Niven's job as deputy to the US Director of Broadcasting, Colonel Ed Kirby, included overseeing the BBC and AEF broadcasts. He is seen here at the microphone during the performance on Thursday, July 13.

Where music and history were both made — the Bedford Corn Exchange as it is today.

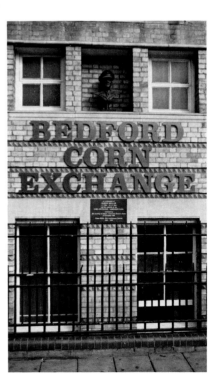

Today, the Corn Exchange, like the control tower at Twinwood Farm airfield just north of the town from where Miller left on his last flight, is reputed to be haunted by his ghost. Many stories of sightings, both in Bedford and the surrounding countryside to the north, carry the legend of Glenn Miller to those who are into that sort of thing. As Glenn's nephew, John Miller, once said, 'It's all good for business!' However, as far as most people are concerned, it's the music and the memory of America's most famous bandleader that counts. *Above:* A plaque was erected within the building on February 25, 1976 by the Glenn Miller Society to commemorate Miller's connection with the Corn Exchange, and a second memorial plaque beneath a bust on the exterior *(right)* during the anniversary year of 1994.

Co-Partners Hall

BEDFORD

Co-Partners Hall, off Havelock Street in Queens Park, on the west side of Bedford, was known by the members of Glenn Miller's orchestra as 'the shack in the field'. It was then Studio No. 4 in Bedford and used as both a rehearsal studio and broadcasting home for the band. Most sub-units from the band broadcast and recorded from here. These included Sergeant Ray McKinley's Swing Shift and Sergeant Mel Powell's Swing Sextet (the Uptown Hall Gang). The *Strings with Wings*, *Piano Parade* and the *Sergeant Johnny Desmond Sings* shows, and even some of the full orchestra programmes, came live from this small building. In order to meet the exacting sound requirements for broadcasting, the band had to use sound-deadening material in the form of cabot quilting (a special type of seaweed sewn between canvas). Sandbags and US Army blankets had to be used as additional wall lining.

Co-Partners Hall played host to many top stars visiting the area. British singers included Anne Shelton (Sunday, July 23), Sam Browne (Thursday, August 3) and Gloria Brent (Thursday, September 7). American singers Dinah Shore (Thursday, August 3) and Bing Crosby (Tuesday, August 29 and Wednesday, August 30) also performed there.

During the period from November 25 to December 12, when the band was stockpiling recordings to cover their transfer to France in December 1944, Co-Partners Hall was used day and night for recording, besides additional live broadcasts.

Studio No. 4 in Bedford, otherwise known to history as Co-Partners Hall [7], is one of the most important venues associated with Glenn Miller. It was here that the bulk of the recordings by both the orchestra and its sub-units were carried out. In addition, other famous personalities made use of its somewhat cramped facilities. In this picture, Bing Crosby, right, is seen examining scripts with Paul Dudley and Glenn Miller during a break in recording a *Bing Crosby Sings* programme. Not only can we place the date precisely — August 30 — but also the time: to between 1.30 and 3.30 p.m.!

A somewhat more formal occasion. Miller and the American Band of the AEF with British guest star Gloria Brent during the live BBC-AEF programme broadcast from Co-Partners Hall on the evening of Thursday, September 7.

Above: Glenn and the band's arranger, Sergeant Jerry Gray, left, relax on the grass outside Co-Partners Hall during a break in the busy schedule in August 1944. Jerry was an old friend of Glenn's, having been an arranger and composer with his civilian bands before the war. To him fell the onerous task of directing the band in Paris on Christmas Day after Glenn's disappearance was announced. *Right:* Today, the wall in the background has been incorporated into bicycle sheds. The area was originally part of Bedford Town Football Club but was redeveloped by the Charles Wells Brewery in 1976. *Below left:* Fortunately, the company retained Co-Partners Hall as the works' canteen *(below right)* — a fitting use bearing in mind its former connection with the entertainment world. The rear part of the building is used for the reception of deliveries for the brewery.

Granada Cinema

BEDFORD

The Granada Cinema in St Peter's Street, Bedford, was the special venue for the Eighth Air Force's 'Carnival of Bands' held by the VIII Air Force Service Command on the afternoon of Sunday, November 26, 1944. American film star, Lieutenant Colonel Ben Lyon, famous for his *Hi Gang* radio programme on the BBC, organised the whole event and even invited his old radio friend Vic Oliver to be one of the judges. From our point of view, the most important judge was Glenn Miller who was billeted just along the road in the American Red Cross Officer's Club.

Also on hand were the bands from the four Strategic Air Depots of the Eighth Air Force. Respectively, the bands were known as 'The Yanks', from the 1st SAD at Honington; 'The Gremlins', from the 2nd SAD at Abbots Ripton; 'The Continentals', from the 3rd SAD at Watton; and 'The High Flyers', from the 4th SAD at Wattisham. All came under the VIII Service Command headquarters at Milton Ernest Hall, about four miles north of Bedford.

Other guests taking part in this event included Teddy Brown, June Manton and Betty Paul. Photographs of the proceedings were taken by Louis Lawrence. At the end of the 'Carnival of Bands', Miller conducted all four SAD bands with a finale of the *Army Air Corps Song*, *The Star Spangled Banner* and *God Save the King*. It was by all accounts a very cold afternoon as Glenn wore an air force 'Parka' throughout the concert.

Above left: **Seen here in 1970, the Granada [8] in St Peter's Street, Bedford, was opened in 1934 at the height of the cinema age. It was demolished in 1991 to make way for a new office development which, in the event, never materialised and the site currently remains an empty plot** (*above right*).

Program

ORGAN	Christmas Music	JOHN UFF
INTRODUCTION		Lt. HARRY H. BLOOM
MASTER OF CEREMONIES		Lt. Col. BEN LYON
FIRST ORCHESTRA	YANKS of First Strategic Air Depot	

Director and Vocalist: T/Sgt. JACK MANWELL

VIC OLIVER and JUNE MANTON

SECOND ORCHESTRA — GREMLINS of Second Strategic Air Depot
Director: Pfc. LYMAN WOOD
Vocalist: Sgt. RAYMOND ARD

TEDDY BROWN

THIRD ORCHESTRA — CONTINENTALS of Third Strategic Air Depot
Director: Sgt. PETER KARA
Vocalist: Pfc. NICK GIAMMURSE

SKETCH ... "The Convict's Return"
WAC Pfc. MAYBELLE POWELL   Cpl. KING DONOVAN

BACK BEAT BOOGIE — CONTINENTALS of Third Strategic Air Depot

Intermission

Act Two

FOURTH ORCHESTRA — HIGH FLYERS of Fourth Strategic Air Depot
Director: Pvt. DICK MOTTER
Vocalist: Pvt. HERSCHEL AYRES

SKETCH ... "Two Individuals"
T/Sgt. GEORGE WALSH   Cpl. LESTER AMPOLSK

JUMP MEDLEY — HIGH FLYERS of Fourth Strategic Air Depot

VIC OLIVER and BETTY PAUL

FINALE ... Four Combined Orchestras
Director: Major GLENN MILLER

ARMY AIR CORPS SONG
STAR SPANGLED BANNER
GOD SAVE THE KING

Acknowledgments

VIC OLIVER   TEDDY BROWN   LT. COL. BEN LYON
MAJOR GLENN MILLER
JUNE MANTON   BETTY PAUL   BRONWEN JONES
Theatre Facilities by GRANADA THEATRES, LTD.
Messrs. E. BLAKE, C. R. R. TINGEY, Directors, Granada (Bedford) Ltd.
H. C. FONTAINE, N. HOBART, G. C. BALDWIN,
Organist: JOHN UFF
Piano by FRASER'S MUSIC STORE
Public Address System by PERFECT ACOUSTICS Mr. MAYES
Program by OFFICERS' CLUB OF HQ., VIII AIR FORCE SERVICE COMMAND
Stage Manager: Lt. HARRY H. BLOOM
Stage Committee: Cpl. KING DONOVAN, Sgt. LEO DIETRICH, Pvt. CHARLES KIRKLAND, Pvt. GEORGE SPELVIN

Above: **An extract from the programme for the Carnival of Bands held on November 26, 1944.** *Below left:* **Major Glenn Miller with Lieutenant Colonel Ben Lyon and a sax player from one of the bands taking part in the carnival.** *Below right:* **Vic Oliver and Ben Lyon with The Gremlins of the 2nd Strategic Air Depot.**

American Red Cross Club

BELFAST, NORTHERN IRELAND

Two shots of the Plaza Ballroom in Belfast as it appeared at the time of the concert. It has since been demolished and a new building erected on the site called, appropriately, Plaza Buildings, which contains various government offices.

Just after lunch on Sunday, August 13, 1944, Captain Glenn Miller and the dance band (minus the string section) of the American Band of the AEF were picked up by two C-47 transport aircraft at RAF Twinwood Farm, just outside Bedford, and flown to the vast Base Air Depot at Langford Lodge, some 15 miles from Belfast, in Northern Ireland. Their flight took 1½ hours. After landing at Langford Lodge, they quickly packed their equipment and instruments into trucks and then were driven by road into Belfast.

Between 4.45 and 5.45 p.m., Miller and the band gave a concert at the American Red Cross Club located in the former Plaza Ball-room in Chichester Street. The club was packed with an audience of 1,200 enlisted personnel and members of the general public. After the concert, the band were transported back directly to Langford Lodge, where, after dinner, they performed for several hundred personnel in the camp cinema (see page 64).

Bentley Priory

STANMORE, MIDDLESEX

Today, Bentley Priory is still an important Royal Air Force headquarters, and is currently the No. 11 Group control centre for the air defence of the UK. Regrettably, no photographs of the concert seem to exist, but this is the lawn behind the mansion where it was held as it appeared in post-war years.

On Wednesday, August 16, the American Band of the AEF, conducted by Glenn Miller, performed a special concert during the afternoon on the lawn behind the Officers' Mess at the RAF Fighter Command HQ at Bentley Priory at Stanmore in north London. A thousand British and American officers and enlisted men attended. While the band was playing its first tune, *In the Mood*, a V1 flying bomb made its appearance. The band continued playing, but more softly, as Miller wanted to make sure he could hear clearly if the motor cut out. Fortunately, it did not and in less than 30 seconds it was out of sight. However, this now-celebrated incident was portrayed in the 1954 Universal Studios film, *The Glenn Miller Story*, with somewhat more dramatic impact!

Bovingdon Station 112

HERTFORDSHIRE

Bovingdon airfield, opened in 1942, was used by the 11th Combat Crew Replacement Unit for B-17 operational training. In September 1944, it was taken over by the European Air Transport Service and, between August 25, 1944 and the end of 1945, the SHAEF shuttle operated by the US Air Transport Command used the airfield. All SHAEF personnel flying to Paris used Bovingdon as their starting point, as did Glenn Miller and Don Haynes.

Although Glenn used Bovingdon on several occasions, the orchestra never performed here. It is included because of its use by the two senior officers of the American Band of the AEF. It was also from this airfield that Glenn Miller should have departed for France on Thursday, December 14, 1944. However, due to the very foggy conditions on that day, all flights were cancelled. This, in turn, caused a backlog of senior personnel trying to get to the Continent. Miller knew he would have to wait ages under this system so when Lieutenant Colonel Norman F. Baessell (an acquaintance of Miller at VIII Air Force Service Command) said he was going to fly out from RAF Twinwood Farm in one of his chief's personal planes, Glenn jumped at the chance, a decision which led directly to his death (see page136).

Apart from Glenn Miller, Bovingdon, seven miles west of Watford, saw many entertainers pass through, including the indefatigable Bob Hope. The airfield closed in 1972 and part of the site is now a prison for young offenders.

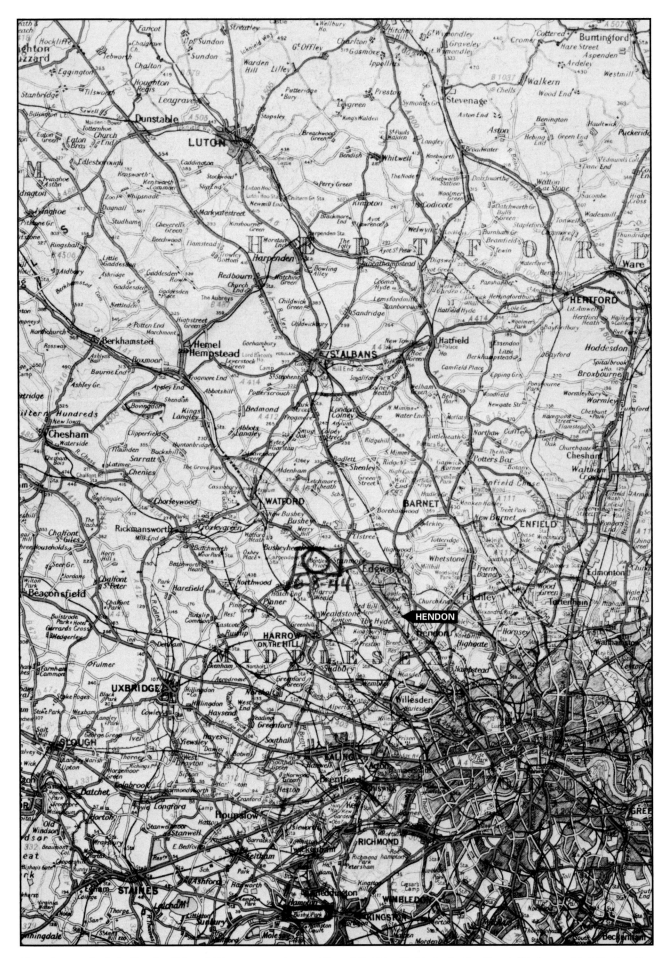

Glenn has marked the Bentley Priory 'V1' concert on August 16 in his atlas and has ringed Bovingdon — the normal departure airfield for flights to the Continent. We have added the location of Hendon (see page 53).

Boxted Station 150

Captain Glenn Miller and the American Band of the AEF perform *In the Mood* for the airmen at Boxted fighter base on Sunday, August 6, 1944.

ESSEX

Late on the afternoon of Sunday, August 6, Miller and the American Band of the AEF gave a concert for the 56th Fighter Group at Boxted airfield, three miles north-west of Colchester, Essex. There they played for 3,000 officers and enlisted personnel in No. 1 Hangar. During the performance, Glenn met Colonel Hubert Zemke (see page 10), the CO of the 56th, destined to become one of the top Eighth Air Force fighter aces of World War II. The orchestra stayed for dinner and then returned to Bedford.

Later that same month, a small dance band, under pianist Staff Sergeant Mel Powell, performed at a special officer's dance at this base on the evening of Saturday, August 19.

Much of Boxted is now an orchard but some of the original buildings around the southern end, by Langford Lodge, remain. However, the site of the hangar where Glenn performed is now occupied by a modern office block.

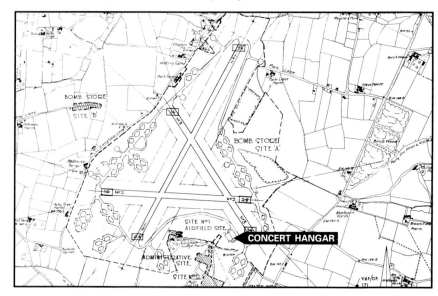

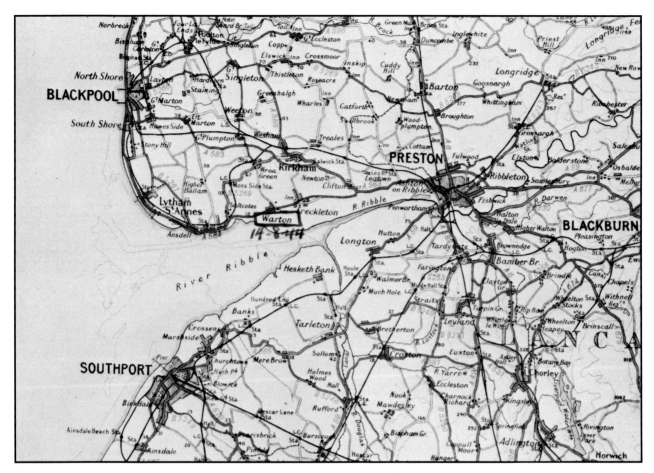

After the band made their whistle-stop visit to Northern Ireland on Sunday, August 13 (see page 31), they flew back to Warton (above) where they spent the night. The following afternoon, they gave a concert for a massed audience at the air base depot before hopping 30 miles to the south on Tuesday to Burtonwood (below). This base was even larger so they had to give both an afternoon and evening performance before flying back to Bedford late that night.

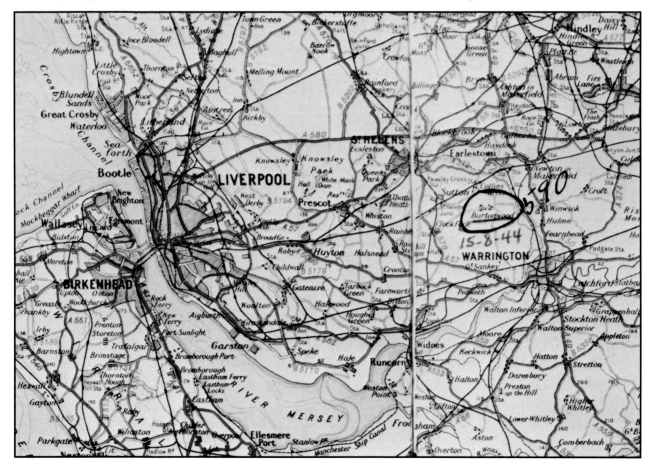

Burtonwood Station 590

Glenn at the microphone during one of the Burtonwood shows — the programme included *That Old Black Magic, Tuxedo Junction, String of Pearls* and *Stealin' Apples*.

LANCASHIRE

Burtonwood airfield, three miles north-west of Warrington (since 1974 in Cheshire), was opened in 1940. It was taken over by the United States Air Service Command and used as a Base Air Depot from early 1942 and by 1944 it had become the largest BAD in Europe.

On August 15, Glenn and the dance band, together with singers of the American Band of the AEF, landed in two B-24s (one was named *Donna Mia*) after their stay the previous day at Warton airfield (see page 132). The band had lunch before performing in a hangar on a stage made out of crated B-17 and B-24 engines. Special British guests who had driven up from London were the bandleader Joe Loss and 'the Force's Sweetheart', Vera Lynn. Glenn Miller played to 8,000 officers and enlisted personnel between 2.30 and 4 p.m.

So vast was Burtonwood, with such a large number of Eighth Air Force personnel, that Miller and the band played a second concert in the same hangar for a further 9,000 at 7 p.m. that evening. After the show was over, Glenn and the band flew back in the same two Liberators to RAF Twinwood Farm but the pilots got lost in the dark and landed in error at nearby Thurleigh. After some embarrassing exchanges with groundcrew, the aircraft quickly took off again for the three-mile hop to Twinwood.

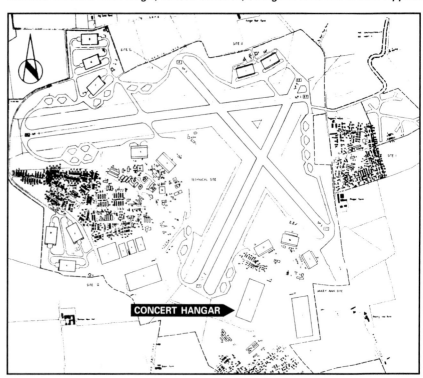

CONCERT HANGAR

Above: **Captain Glenn Miller with British bandleader Joe Loss and Vera Lynn outside the hangar at Base Air Depot No. 1 at Burtonwood, near Warrington, on the afternoon of Tuesday, August 15, 1944. Burtonwood — the largest US base in the United Kingdom during the Second World War — employed over 18,000 American servicemen and women and acted as a co-ordinating centre for the maintenance of aircraft for the Eighth, Ninth, Twelfth and Fifteenth Air Forces. However, coal mining beneath the airfield led to its closure in 1965 although it was maintained as a V-Bomber dispersal base until 1970 and the US still retained control of the huge storage hangar until 1993. It covers an incredible 47 *acres*! The M62 motorway now crosses Burtonwood on the line of the main runway, the former airfield being earmarked for mixed housing and industrial development. Aldon P. Ferguson of the Burtonwood Association kindly took the comparison photographs for us with the co-operation of some of the demolition contractors as little now remains to be seen of the buildings on the airfield itself.**

Don Haynes, Joe Loss, Vera Lynn, Glenn and an unidentified base officer pose for a group shot, ably complemented by our

1995 builder stand-ins! Most of the wartime snapshots were taken by Denver Rice.

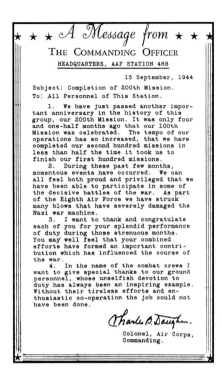

Bury St Edmunds Station 468

SUFFOLK

During the afternoon of Friday, September 15, the American Band of the AEF left Bedford by road transport and headed for the 94th Bomb Group base, three miles east of Bury St Edmunds, near the village of

September 15, 1944 was a day of bad weather with cancelled operations for the Eighth Air Force so the concert by the American Band of the AEF held in No. 1 Hangar at Bury St Edmunds that Friday, was a very welcome interlude.

Rougham, by which name the airfield is also sometimes known. Glenn was unwell with sinus problems and had to stay behind in Bedford.

The concert was held in No. 1 Hangar, from 7.30 to 8.30 p.m. Also appearing with the orchestra was American film and singing star Dinah Shore, who had just returned to the United Kingdom after a six-week United

Service Organization tour of the European Theater of Operations. (The USO, begun in February 1941, was sponsored by several welfare bodies to provide a 'home away from home' for enlisted persons.) Needless to say, Dinah was none too pleased to find that Glenn was absent and that the band was instead to be directed by drummer, Sergeant Ray McKinley.

During the concert, Dinah Shore was presented with a model of a B-17 Flying Fortress.

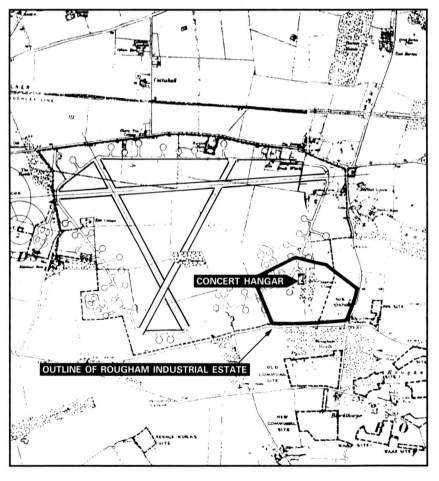

CONCERT HANGAR

OUTLINE OF ROUGHAM INDUSTRIAL ESTATE

Bury St Edmunds remains one of only four locations of Glenn's airfield concerts where the original hangar in which the band performed can still be seen (the others being Framlingham, North Witham and Polebrook). All the others have been demolished — often as part of the resale conditions to landowners post-war. The technical site is now part of the Rougham Trading Estate, the particular T2 hangar concerned having been purchased early in 1995 by Eniti Limited for the storage of tea. However, an on-going refurbishment plan will result in the complete recladding of the original framework.

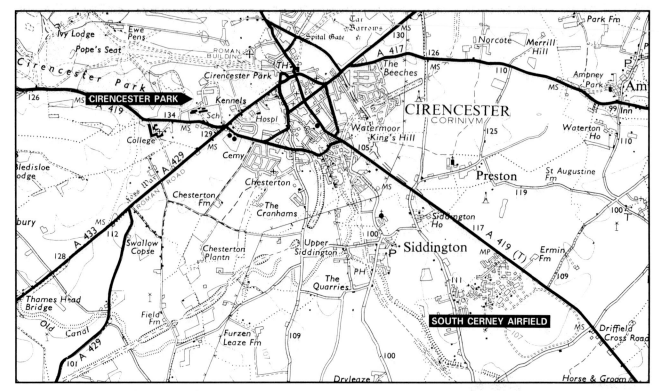

US Army General Hospital

CIRENCESTER, GLOUCESTERSHIRE

During the late morning of Monday, August 7, 1944, Glenn Miller and the dance band and singers of the American Band of the AEF flew in three C-47s from Twinwood Farm to South Cerney airfield, near Cirencester, in Gloucestershire. A concert had been arranged in Cirencester Park for the US 188th and 192nd General Hospitals based there as well as an RAF medical unit. The band were driven from the airfield in coaches to the park to the west of Cirencester.

The first concert was held in the open and attended by an audience of around 3,500 patients, nurses and doctors. Afterwards, Glenn broke up the band into several sub-units which played in all the wards for those too ill to be moved outside. Later during the evening, Miller and the band gave a second concert, this time for an audience estimated at 4,000.

The route taken by Glenn and the band from South Cerney airfield to the concert site in Cirencester Park (home of the US 188th and 192nd General Hospitals) was undoubtedly straight up the A419. The map *(top)* shows the relationship of both locations. *Right:* Although little evidence of the old hospital buildings remains, fortunately two of the 192nd Nissen huts, visible in the concert photograph *(centre),* still stand, providing a ghostly link with the past. Bill King of the Ridgeway Military and Aviation Research Group supplied the contemporary photographs and took the comparisons. Other odd buildings still remain like the guardhouse which was still in use as a private residence up until 1990. A fence divided the two hospital sites but whereas the 192nd area has reverted to agriculture, that of the 188th is now occupied by Deer Park School. There was another US hospital north of Cirencester near Stratton and it is said that some of the more mobile patients were brought down to the concert given by Glenn's American Band of the AEF on August 7, 1944.

The concert gets underway against a leafy backdrop.

The same field today as seen from the boundary fence.

Above: **These photographs were taken by one of the NCOs of the 192nd General Hospital and given to his English girlfriend who attended the afternoon concert in Cirencester Park .**

Below left: **Captain Glenn Miller hitches up his pants during the show.** *Below right:* **Now just the corner of another field but one where a legend once performed.**

41

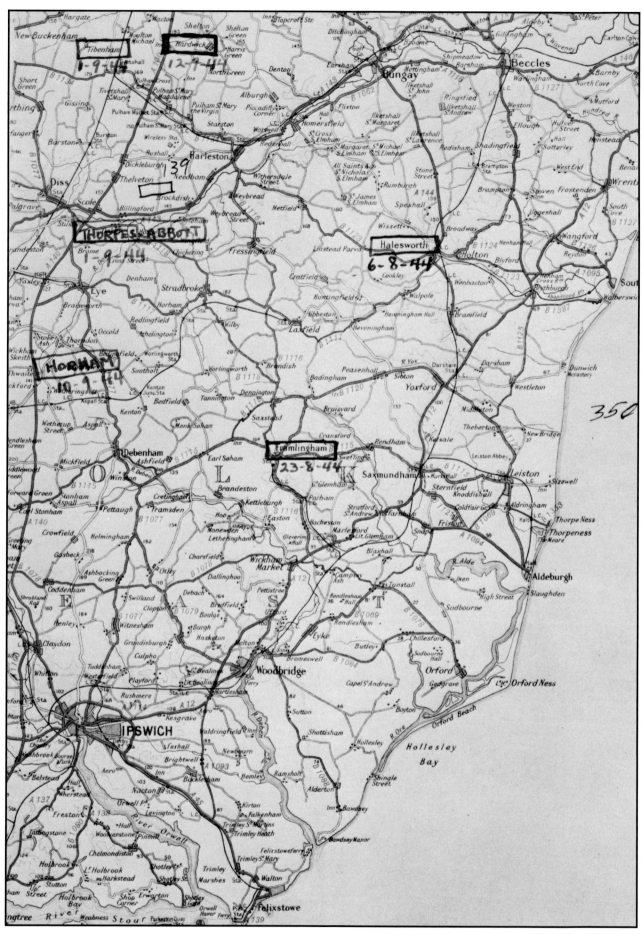

The East Anglian airbase concerts. It would appear that Glenn entered the dates on his map after they had performed because Hardwick was originally due to be given on August 29 (see page 52). Above the date for Thorpe Abbotts (Station 139) he has drawn a small square indicating the actual position of the airfield just west of Brockdish.

Of all the East Anglian airfields at which the orchestra played, Framlingham is one of the most fortunate with the tower beautifully restored as a memorial to the 390th Bomb Group.

The T2 hangar seen in the background, where the concert was performed, is still retained by the Ministry of Defence in its original, albeit now somewhat rusty, condition.

Framlingham Station 153

SUFFOLK

Framlingham, three miles south-east of the village of the same name, was built in 1942-43 and after a short tenure by the 95th Bomb Group in May 1943, it became the home of the 390th Bomb Group from August until the end of the war. It is sometimes also known as Parham, because the airfield lies much closer to that village.

On the evening of August 23, Glenn Miller and the entire American Band of the AEF played in No. 2 Hangar at the 100th mission party given by the 390th. The group had actually carried out their 100th operation over three months earlier — on May 8 to Berlin before Glenn Miller had even arrived in the UK — so the presence of the band that Wednesday undoubtedly, made the celebration party something special.

The music stands were mounted on a makeshift bandstand built up with straw bales and some 6,000 attended the combined concert and dance held between 7.15 p.m. and 9.45 p.m. Afterwards, there was a party for Glenn and the band in the 390th Officers' Club.

The orchestra stayed at Framlingham overnight and, in the early hours of the following morning, Glenn and Don Haynes were invited to attend an aircrew briefing.

The somewhat rural setting for the band's Framlingham concert is plainly evident in this shot of Glenn conducting at the evening show in No. 2 Hangar. At least everyone performing got to attend a party in more salubrious surroundings afterwards! According to Don Haynes diary, both he and Glenn were awoken early the following morning to attend a briefing for a raid on Schweinfurt. However, no such operation took place; in fact, the 390th did not fly at all on either August 23 or 24!

A contemporary view of the Officers' Club, where Glenn and Don Haynes had dinner, taken two months after their visit.

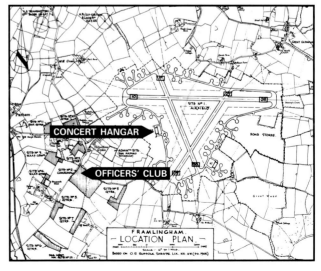

CONCERT HANGAR

OFFICERS' CLUB

FRAMLINGHAM.
- LOCATION PLAN. -

Member of Parliament for Grantham, W. Denis Kendall, introduces Major Glenn Miller's American Band of the AEF to the audience at the State Theatre on Sunday, September 24, 1944.

State Theatre

GRANTHAM, LINCOLNSHIRE

After the concert for airborne troops held at North Witham on September 24 (see page 100), Glenn and the band travelled some 8½ miles north up the A1 (the Great North Road, as it was then known) to Grantham. Between 3 and 4 p.m., they gave a concert, organised by the local Member of Parliament, W. Denis Kendall, at the State Theatre on St Peter's Hill. The State was a relatively large theatre for a place like Grantham and was packed to overflowing with 1,500 American servicemen, munitions workers and townsfolk. As the concert was a charity event, entry was free on a first come, first served basis and many people in the huge crowd had queued for up to four hours. Because so many could not get in, it was relayed to those outside on the Green.

In 1954, the State became the Granada but, like so many cinemas, it was destined to become the victim of television and it closed in 1987, being demolished the following year. The site was subsequently redeveloped and is currently occupied by the Alliance & Leicester Building Society.

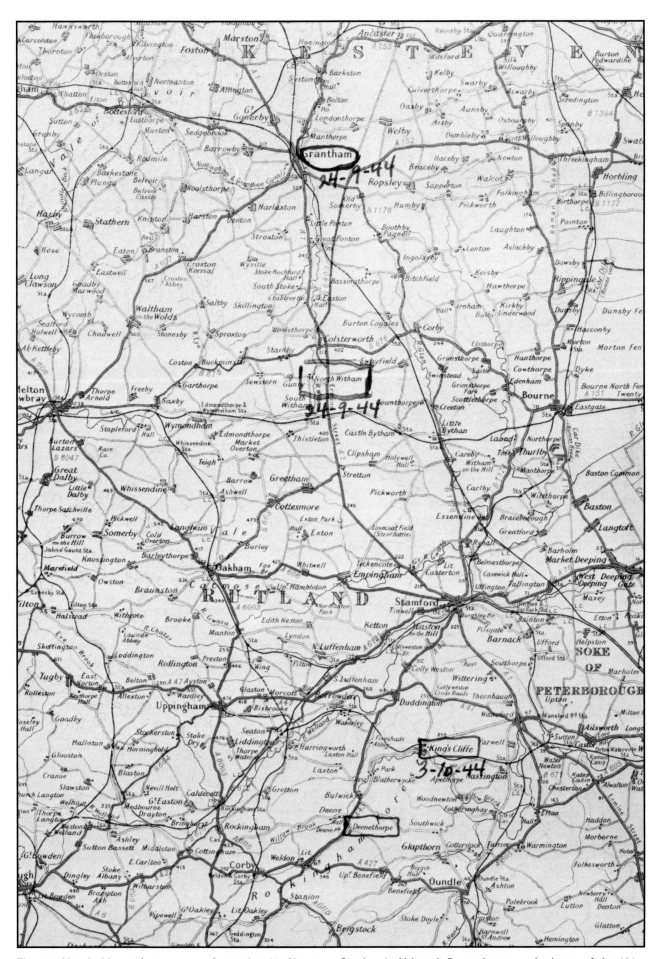

The two Lincolnshire performances on September 24. Also on this map is Kingscliffe, the last of the airfield concerts held on October 3. Although Deenethorpe — the home of the 401st Bomb Group — is also marked, the band never played there.

By the autumn of 1944, several Eighth Air Force Bomb Groups were nearing 200 operations and the 385th at Great Ashfield planned to celebrate it in grand style although their actual 200th mission (to Cologne on October 17) was yet to take place.

There were no ops at all for the 385th on Sunday, October 1 and dozens of girls were brought up from London to enjoy the party. This shot of Paula Green struggling to entertain the troops comes from her own album — note her muddy frock!

Great Ashfield Station 155

SUFFOLK

The Eighth Air Force airfield at Great Ashfield, also known as Elmswell, ten miles east of Bury St Edmunds, was the home of the 385th Bomb Group. It was opened in 1943 and personnel of the 385th moved in on June 19, the group becoming known as 'Van's Valiants' after their first CO, Colonel Elliott Vandevanter.

Celebrating their 200th mission with a grand party on Sunday, October 1, 1944, Major Glenn Miller's American Band of the AEF, conducted by Sergeant Ray McKinley, were asked to play at the event held in No. 1 Hangar. British singing star Paula Green from the Geraldo Orchestra and the BBC's *ITMA* [It's That Man Again] programme was also a participant.

Also attending was the Commanding General of the Eighth Air Force, General James Doolittle, who later wrote that 'at Great Ashfield in Suffolk, I attended a 200 mission party in October of 1944 where there was an audience of 15,000. The amplification system on the stage in the vast hangar went dead a few minutes before the concert and, without the aid of microphones, the men beyond the first few rows heard nothing.'

'And that wasn't all,' recalls Paula Green, 'because before the show some of the boys had insisted on taking me on a merry-go-round at a fair and I'd fallen off and got my frock filthy. There I stood in my dirty frock on the stage in the hangar, singing to an audience that couldn't hear a sound. They kept whistling and stomping and who could blame them? Then, when they got the mikes working and I was well away with a good old sentimental song, somebody's little dog got loose and ran around the stage. That was not a successful day!'

Nevertheless, 15 minutes of the first one-hour concert (from 3.30 to 4.30 p.m.) were broadcast to the USA. Sergeant Ray McKinley and the band then gave a second performance in the same hangar at 8 p.m.

When the Miles family purchased the airfield in 1960, John Miles desperately wanted to keep the hangar but it was a condition that all the buildings had to be dismantled. Thus only the concrete base remains to be seen today as a reminder of Great Ashfield's greatest-ever party.

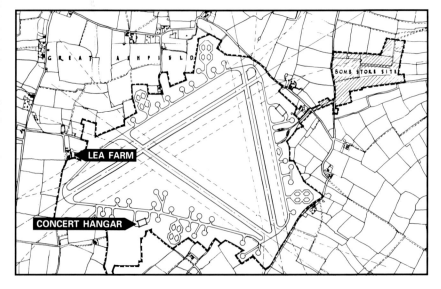

In spite of an exhaustive search, no photos of the band at Greenham Common on July 25, 1944 have come to light. However, in October 1995, a special 'Goodbye Greenham' concert, dedicated to all those who had served at the base during World War II,

was given by the Herb Miller Orchestra, conducted by John Miller *(right)*. The band played in the Liberty Ballroom, the post-war gymnasium-cum-leisure centre, located not that far from where John's uncle had performed. Pictures by Les Newport.

Greenham Common
Station 486

BERKSHIRE

The airfield at Greenham Common, two miles south-east of Newbury, Berkshire was opened in 1942 as the headquarters of the 51st Troop Carrier Wing until their move to

North Africa in November the same year. After nine months with RAF Training Command, Greenham was taken over by Ninth Air Force for the headquarters of the 53rd Troop Carrier Wing. The 438th Troop Carrier Group arrived on March 16 and led the Ninth troop carrier force on D-Day.

On the afternoon of Tuesday, July 25, Glenn Miller and the American Band of the AEF were picked up from Twinwood Farm in three C-47 transport planes of the 438th Troop Carrier Group. Don Haynes noted in

his diary for that day that the aircraft were nicknamed *Skylark*, *Patches*, and *Patsy Ann*.

Upon arrival at Greenham Common, Glenn and the orchestra gave a two-hour concert before an audience of 2,500 officers, enlisted men and WACs gathered together in a marquee which had been erected on the technical site.

Glenn and the band stayed for dinner before being taken in trucks and a Jeep to nearby Newbury for a second concert at the Corn Exchange (see page 99).

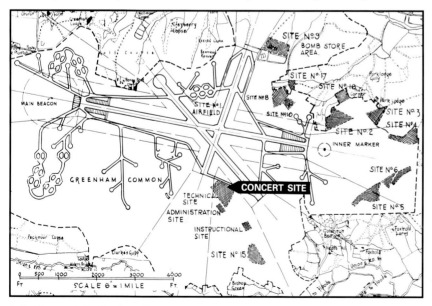

Left: Glenn originally played in a marquee set up near the static water tower on the technical site on the south side of the airfield. After the war, Greenham Common was retained by the USAF, becoming one of the front line bases of the Strategic Air Command. However, its layout was dramatically changed with

the construction of a massive new E-W runway which involved the complete demolition of the wartime technical site although the main camp road was still retained. *Right:* This present-day aerial shot looks north along the road [1] past the Liberty Ballroom [2] on the left to the site of the 1944 concert [3].

Grove Station 519

BERKSHIRE

The airfield at Grove, just north of Wantage, was built in 1941-42 and opened that October being used by the IX Air Force Air Service Command as a Tactical Air Depot, repairing, in the main, A-20 Havoc and P-61 Black Widow aircraft. In October 1943, the AFSC formed its own air transport unit, the 31st Transport Group, flying C-47 transport aircraft.

On Saturday, August 12, 1944, a small jazz group of seven musicians, under pianist Staff Sergeant Mel Powell, played during the evening at the Officers' Club dance held for the 31st TG at Grove. This was the only concert given by Glenn Miller's American Band of the AEF at this base.

There seems to be some confusion as to just what happened at the August 12 concert at Grove. Diaries and personal recollections of members of the band point to Mel Powell's small dance band playing in the Officers' Mess. However, local legend indicates split performances by the full band playing in the gymnasium and in the open air between the gym and the western end of the E-W runway. Undoubtedly, people are confusing other concerts given by different bands but this case illustrates vividly the confusion that has arisen over the years with wartime big band concerts. Everyone who saw an American band in uniform perform, seemed to regard it as a Glenn Miller concert!

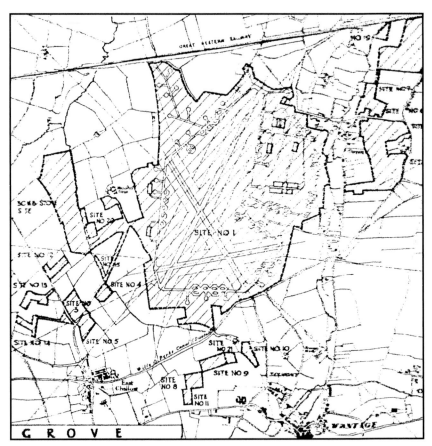

Grove today. Both the gymnasium and the Officers' Mess were located on Site No. 2, which lay just off the southern perimeter (on the right in this photo), now occupied by the works of the Metal Box Company.

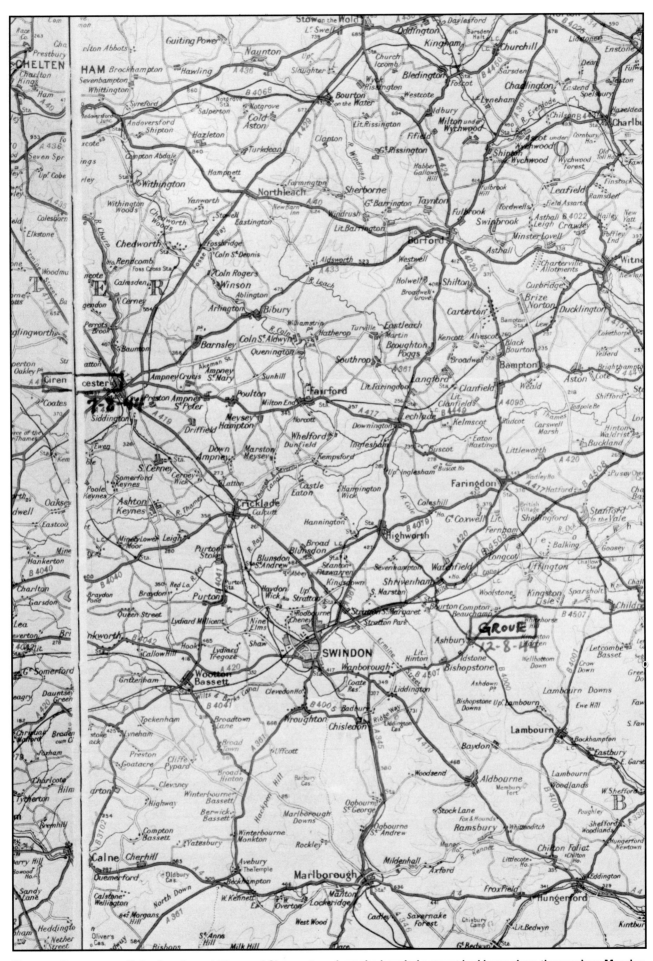

Grove — the venue on Saturday, August 12 — and Cirencester where the hospital concert had been given the previous Monday.

Halesworth Station 365

SUFFOLK

Captain Miller and the dance band play *In the Mood* for 489th Bomb Group personnel grouped on and around a B-24 in the main hangar at Halesworth on August 6. The original 'Star and Bar' insignia on the music stands brought over from the States was crudely replaced with the SHAEF badge over the weekend of July 22-23.

Halesworth airfield, built near the village of Holton, was opened in July 1943. It was one of the most easterly Eighth Air Force airfields, being only eight miles west of Southwold on the Suffolk coast. Halesworth was first used by the 56th Fighter Group, equipped with P-47 Thunderbolts and led by Colonel Hubert Zemke, but in April 1944 the 56th Fighter Group had to vacate the airfield to make way for the 489th Bomb Group, flying B-24 Liberators, which were operational by the end of May.

On Sunday, August 6, Glenn Miller and the dance band unit from the orchestra were picked up from Twinwood Farm by two B-24s based at Halesworth to be flown to the 56th Fighter Group's new airfield at Boxted near Colchester for a concert (see page 34). According to the 489th Bomb Group history, the Group CO, Colonel Ezekiel W. Napier, had made it a condition of the supply of the aircraft that Miller play at his base. However, members of the band remember it somewhat differently in that it was only when they were airborne, en route for Boxted, that the pilot asked Glenn why he was not going to perform at his base at Halesworth. Glenn said to his Executive Officer, Don Haynes, 'Haynesie, why not?' The pilot then asked the radio operator to make a quick call to the control tower at Halesworth to organise the reception and the three bombers quickly changed course and headed east.

After landing, the dance band quickly set up in the main (No. 1) hangar, still containing several Liberators. One was rolled outside and the music stands were placed on a flat-bed trailer. Captain Miller and the dance band then gave their famous 'Hunk O'Home' medley for an hour for the 1,500 members of the 489th.

Directly afterwards, Miller and the band quickly packed their gear and took off in the same three aircraft for Boxted.

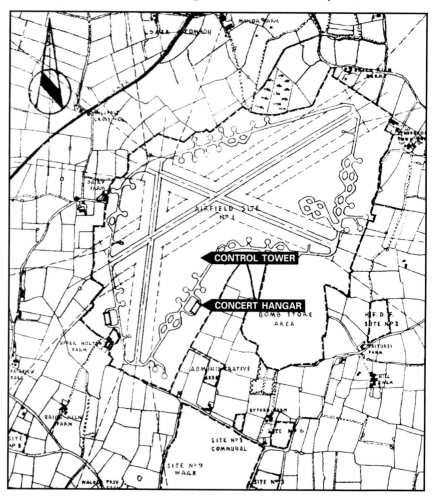

Halesworth was sold off in 1946 and was one of the first airfield sites acquired by Bernard Matthews for his burgeoning turkey business. While large turkey sheds adorn the runways, the site of the hangar used for the concert now lies within the modern meat processing plant. The company prefers to keep a low profile to avoid the attentions of animal rights agitators, and no photography is permitted, but it was confirmed to us that the effluent plant is now sited where the hangar once stood. We therefore dug in our archives and pulled out this comparison we took in 1978 before the new factory was built.

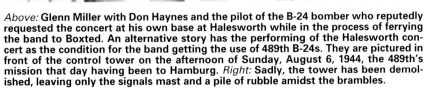

Above: Glenn Miller with Don Haynes and the pilot of the B-24 bomber who reputedly requested the concert at his own base at Halesworth while in the process of ferrying the band to Boxted. An alternative story has the performing of the Halesworth concert as the condition for the band getting the use of 489th B-24s. They are pictured in front of the control tower on the afternoon of Sunday, August 6, 1944, the 489th's mission that day having been to Hamburg. *Right:* Sadly, the tower has been demolished, leaving only the signals mast and a pile of rubble amidst the brambles.

SITE OF HANGAR ►

Hardwick Station 104

NORFOLK

Hardwick airfield, some five miles west of Bungay, was opened in the summer of 1942. It was quickly taken over that November from the 310th Bomb Group of the Eighth Air Force by the 93rd, a B-24 group, known as the 'Travelling Circus' although they remained at Hardwick for the rest of the war.

On Tuesday, September 12, the group's Liberators were out on operations to north-west Germany. Later, between 6.30 p.m. and 7.45 p.m. that evening, Major Glenn Miller and the American Band of the AEF entertained some 3,800 officers and enlisted personnel of the 93rd in a very cold hangar open at both ends; so cold that the band had to wear woollen gloves whilst playing! This concert was to have been held at 3 p.m. on Tuesday, August 29, but had to be rescheduled. (It is just possible that the other concert which had to be cancelled for that Tuesday, which was to have been given to the 55th Fighter Group at Wormingford, Essex, could have been rescheduled for September 12. However, there is no mention of it taking place in group records and none of the ex-members of the 55th that we contacted had

Hardwick closed in 1962 and, with most of the buildings and runways now dismantled, the airfield has reverted to agriculture.

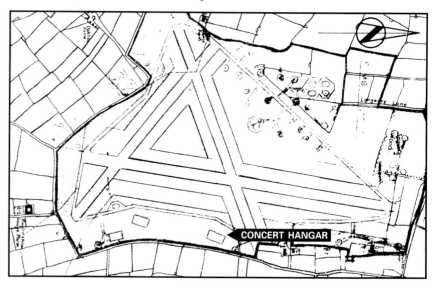

CONCERT HANGAR ►

any recollection of a Miller concert being held at their base.) Miller and the band stayed at Hardwick overnight returning to Bedford the following day.

There are a few of the base concerts for which we could not trace any photographs and, unfortunately, Hardwick is one of them. However, with the help of a wartime plan, we plotted the precise spot where the hangar used for the concert once stood; now an arable field belonging to nearby Burlington Lodge Farm.

Hendon Station 575

MIDDLESEX

Above: **This 1943 shot of Hendon shows the airfield much as it would have appeared when Glenn had his near miss here the following year.** *Below:* **The site has since been developed as the Grahame Park housing estate seen here under construction in 1971. The RAF Museum now occupies some of the old hangars.**

The RAF aerodrome at Hendon is included here, not because Glenn held a concert there, but because of a very frightening incident that occurred on Wednesday, August 16, 1944. This was the day before Glenn was promoted to the rank of major when the American Band of the AEF were scheduled to play at the RAF Headquarters at Bentley Priory (see page 32). The band went by road from Bedford to Stanmore but Miller and Haynes flew down. In the light of what happened a few months later, the incident at Hendon might be considered an ominous portent of things to come — it certainly did not endear Glenn to flying!

As their plane was about to land at Hendon (which was also used by a US transport group), red flares suddenly shot up around them, being the signal to abort. By that time, the aircraft was barely a hundred feet off the ground but the pilot managed to pull the plane up so they could go round again. Although they had been cleared to land, a B-17 was taking off at the same time, and they were about to touch down either immediately in front of or on top of the bomber. As Don Haynes noted in his diary: 'It just about scared the pants off us!' Incidents like this made Miller nervously pace around smoking cigarettes before flying.

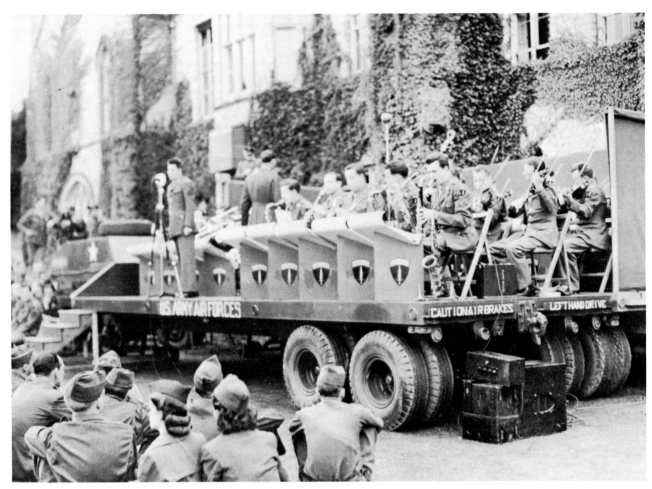

High Wycombe Station 101

Captain Glenn Miller directs the American Band of the Supreme Allied Command as Sergeant Johnny Desmond sings *I'll Get By* during the concert held at Camp Lynn.

BUCKINGHAMSHIRE

Wycombe Abbey, code-named 'Pinetree', at High Wycombe, Buckinghamshire, was the command headquarters of the United States Eighth Air Force; at that time the largest air force in the world, comprising over 200,000 officers and men. Its commander in 1944 was Lieutenant General James H. Doolittle, already famous for his carrier-borne B-25 bombing raid against Japan in 1942. The main headquarters centred around the Abbey, a former school for girls (see *After the Battle* No. 87), and within the 200-acre grounds, an underground operations block had been built which regularly controlled raids of up to 2,000 bombers and 1,000 fighters operating from 50 to 60 airfields. On any one day, there could be up to 21,000 men in the air.

On Saturday, July 29, 1944, at 5.45 p.m., General Doolittle opened the 'V-8' War Bond rally in the grounds of the headquarters which had the official title of Camp Lynn. Following his speech, and the purchase of war bonds to help 'Back the Attack', Glenn Miller gave the downbeat into *Moonlight Serenade*, followed by hit after hit, played from the back of a flat-bed trailer set up facing the school's playing fields. After the concert, Doolittle made his now-famous remark to Glenn that 'next to a letter from home, your music is the greatest morale-booster in the ETO [European Theater of Operations]'.

General Doolittle giving his speech at the opening of the special War Bond rally at his headquarters at High Wycombe on Saturday, July 29, 1944. This particular concert was filmed by cameramen from the Army Air Force (see Frontispiece).

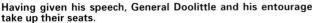

Having given his speech, General Doolittle and his entourage take up their seats.

With the concert now well underway, Glenn plays a muted trombone solo, watched by the string section.

It is believed that Glenn Miller stayed overnight as a guest of General Doolittle at his quarters, some 30 minutes drive from Pinetree. Detailed research by local military historian, Nigel Dawe, pinpointed Quarry Wood Hall *(above)* as the residence in question which has recently been completely refurbished as five exclusive riverside apartments beside the Thames at Marlow. Wycombe Abbey reverted to its pre-war use as a girls' school in 1946 and, although the Nissen huts erected in the grounds have been dismantled, the Abbey itself remains much as it was during the war with a plaque marking Doolittle's former office, now a classroom. *Above right*: Forty-four years later, on Sunday, July 24, 1988, the performance was re-created by the Herb Miller Concert Orchestra directed by Glenn's nephew, John Miller, an idea brought to life by the late Douglas Le-Vicki of the Glenn Miller Society. *Right*: Then, six years later, to mark the 50th anniversary of Glenn Miller's tour of the United Kingdom, the Herb Miller Orchestra, did it all again. Special guest stars were clarinet player Michael 'Peanuts' Hucko and British singing star Gloria Brent, both of whom had performed with Glenn during the war. As with the very first concert, the re-enactments were played on similar flat-bed trailers parked on the same spot as in 1944.

Horham Station 119

With no operations to interfere with their celebrations, the 95th Bomb Group opened their 200th mission party with this impressive display of weaponry.

SUFFOLK

Horham was one of the first heavy bomber airfields built at the beginning of the Second World War in east Suffolk. Located beside the B1117 road to Eye, it was originally destined for the RAF, but when finished it was taken over by the 47th Bomb Group on October 5, 1942. The 95th Bomb Group replaced them on June 15, 1943, completing a total of 320 missions from Horham before the end of hostilities.

On Sunday, September 10, 1944, the 95th celebrated its 200th mission (which had been carried out to Husum in north Germany on August 27) by throwing a major party, and at 6 p.m. Glenn Miller and the American Band of the AEF struck up the opening notes of a combined concert and a dance for 6,500 officers, enlisted personnel and guests in the easternmost of the two T2 hangars.

The American Band of the AEF during the concert at Horham on the evening of September 10, 1944.

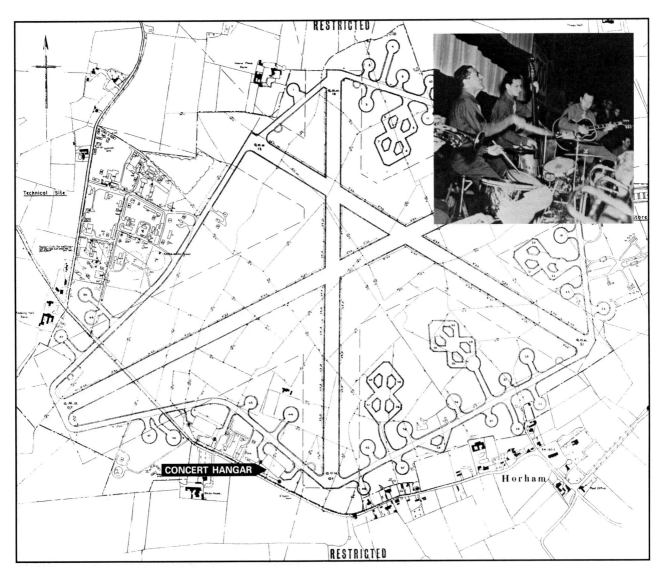

A 1944 plan of Horham with the hangar marked where drummer Ray McKinley *(inset)* kicked up a storm during the show.

After the 95th Bomb Group moved out in August 1945, Horham was taken back by the Royal Air Force, being finally closed down in October 1948. Today, the airfield has reverted to farmland, but the base of the dismantled T2 hangar, just 20 yards from the road, remains almost as good as it was back in 1944.

As we took this comparison, the sweet sound of *Moonlight Serenade* drifted across the old airfield from our pocket tape recorder; an evocative reminder of the day when the Glenn Miller orchestra played for the 95th Bomb Group party on this very spot.

Kimbolton Station 117

British vocalist Dorothy Carless sings while Glenn conducts the American Band of the AEF at Kimbolton on Wednesday, August 2, 1944.

NORTHAMPTONSHIRE

Kimbolton airfield was another of the early bomber airfields built in 1941 for RAF use. Transferred to the Eighth Air Force in September 1942, it was earmarked for the 91st Bomb Group. However, their commander took one look at the sea of mud before transferring his force to Bassingbourn. Further work took place to improve the airfield and upgrade its runways for heavy bomber use and, by late November 1942, the most successful of all the Eighth's bomber units, the 379th, moved in remaining here until May 1945.

Glenn Miller and the dance band ensemble from the American Band of the AEF (which had just been renamed on the orders of General Eisenhower from its original title of the American Band of the Supreme Allied Command) played at Kimbolton on the afternoon of Wednesday, August 2, 1944.

With no operations for the 379th scheduled for that day, Glenn and the band gave two concerts during the afternoon which also featured British singing star Dorothy Carless. The programme was as follows: *Moonlight Serenade* (opening theme); *In the Mood*; *Rhapsody in Blue*; *What do you do in the Infantry?* — vocal, Johnny Desmond and The Crew Chiefs; *A String of Pearls*; *I'll Get by* — vocal, Johnny Desmond; *That Old Black Magic* — vocal, Johnny Desmond; *Star Dust*; *It Must be Jelly*; *Tuxedo Junction*; *American Patrol*; *I Couldn't Sleep a Wink Last Night* — vocal, Dorothy Carless; *Begin the Beguine* — vocal, Dorothy Carless; *Song of the Volga Boatmen*; *Cow Cow Boogie* — vocal, Ray McKinley; *GI Jive* — vocal, Ray McKinley and The Crew Chiefs; *Down the Road a-piece* — vocal, Ray McKinley; and *Anvil Chorus*.

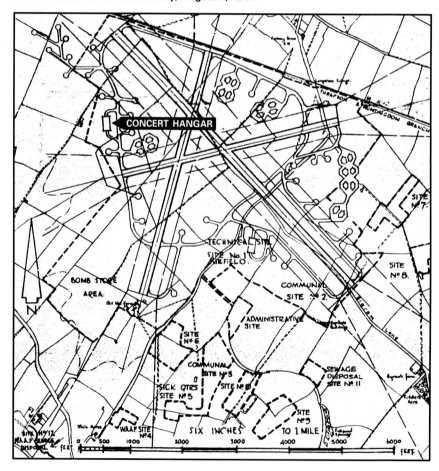

Today, Kimbolton, eight miles west of Huntingdon, has mostly reverted to agriculture while the old technical site has been developed into an industrial estate. Normally at these airfield concerts, the orchestra would play in the main hangar but, in this case, the concert was held in Hangar No. 2 on the far side of the field. Peggy Horsford still recalls clearly the excitement of that day when she learned that Glenn Miller was coming to play at the airfield. Then, she was a 20-year-old voluntary member of the American Red Cross at the base; now, the wife of Ray Convine who owns and farms this part of the airfield. In September 1995, Peggy kindly drove out with us to show us the spot where the hangar once stood.

'It's Chesterfield Time' for Captain Glenn Miller *(above)*, as he pauses to light up while waiting for the band to unload their instruments outside the hangar on the north-west side of the airfield, before announcing the start of the show *(right)*.

Kingscliffe Station 367

NORTHAMPTONSHIRE

Kingscliffe, 12 miles west of Peterborough, was opened in 1941 as a fighter airfield for the RAF and taken over by the 20th Fighter Group of the US Eighth Air Force in August 1943, being the most northerly and westerly of all the Eighth's fighter bases. During the build-up for the Normandy invasion, the 20th Fighter Group were extremely active, flying not only long-range fighter cover with their P-38 Lightnings, but also sorties over the intended landing beaches. They converted to P-51 Mustangs in July the same year.

On Tuesday, October 3, 1944, Glenn and the band travelled by road to Kingscliffe. Just after arrival at the base, Glenn bumped straight into a guy from his past; a family friend, Sergeant Raymond C. Fray, who had dated Glenn's sister Irene at High School in Denver, Colorado.

Earlier that day, the 20th had been out over north-west Germany on escort duties, but they returned in time to enjoy Major Miller and the 40-piece American Band of the AEF giving what was to be the band's last base concert in the British Isles, which lasted from 3 to 4 p.m. in the Callendar Hamilton hangar before an audience of 2,500.

Tuesday, October 3, 1944. Major Miller directs the American Band of the AEF as The Crew Chiefs sing during the last airfield concert held by the orchestra in the UK before the onset of winter put paid to further performances in unheated hangars.

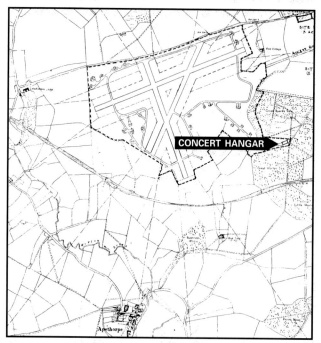

CONCERT HANGAR

Behind the Callendar Hamilton hangar at Kingscliffe, Major Glenn Miller talks to Sergeant Raymond C. Fray who had dated his sister Irene at High School. Fray was a member of the 446th Air Service Group, attached to the 20th Fighter Group.

The 20th did not return home to the USA until October 1945 when Kingscliffe (on maps it appears as King's Cliffe although the Americans invariably preferred one word) was taken back by the RAF, the station finally closing in January 1959. Local rumour, reinforced by recent newspaper articles, indicate that the concert was held in the camp theatre/cinema, now part of Woodlands Equestrian Centre at Leedsgate Farm on the northern side of the old Roman Road between Wansford and Kingscliffe, a legend that the proprietor freely admits is good for business. However, the concert was actually held in the hangar which once stood at the extreme south-east of the airfield, now within the perimeter of the KSR International works site for the manufacture of the raw material for refractory linings. Fortunately, quarrying of the silica clay has not affected this particular corner, the hangar base remaining virtually intact amid a peaceful woodland setting.

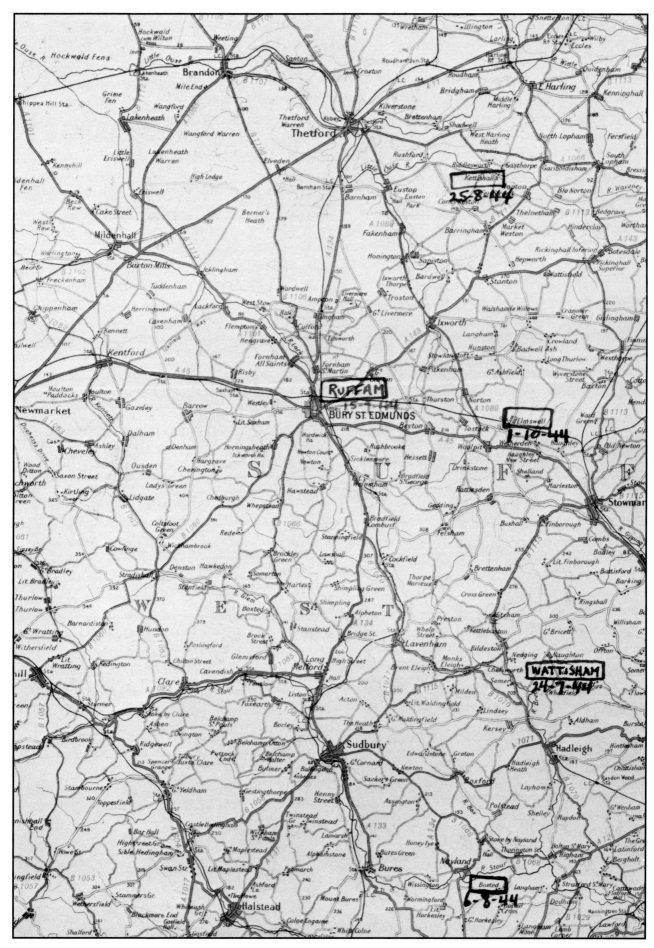

As well as Knettishall, concerts on this page cover July, August, September and October. Glenn calls Bury St Edmunds by its alternative name but spells it phonetically 'Ruffam'. Elmswell is the other name for Great Ashfield.

Knettishall Station 136

SUFFOLK

Glenn Miller plays with the American Band of the AEF during the concert held for the 388th Bomb Group at Knettishall on Friday evening, August 25, 1944.

Knettishall airfield, some five miles east-south-east of Thetford, was built in 1942-43 and was used exclusively by a single Eighth unit: the 388th Bomb Group, flying B-17s.

On Friday evening, August 25, 1944, the American Band of the AEF, led by Glenn Miller, gave a concert and dance in the main hangar for 7,000 officers, enlisted men and guests. Earlier that day, the group had lost one of their B-17s on an operation to Pölitz

The band performed in the southernmost T2 hangar but nothing now remains to indicate where musical history was made.

Even the concrete has been completely removed, the site being occupied in September 1995 by a derelict timber yard.

Frozen on film, this memorable scene recalls a memorable evening enjoyed by the men of the 388th at their Suffolk airbase.

(now Police in Poland). The band stayed at this base overnight, and the following morning Miller and some of the musicians were flown back to Twinwood Farm in one of the Knettishall B-17s, appropriately named *Moonlight Serenade*. Like Miller, this B-17G was lost before the war's end — in this case, during a raid on the Daimler-Benz factory at Stuttgart on September 5, 1944.

Glenn with pilot Richard D. Richard, and his specially-named B-17G *Moonlight Serenade* at Knettishall on Saturday morning, August 26. This Fortress, serial 43-37599 Q-Queen, was on the strength of the 562nd Bomb Squadron when it was shot down just ten days later while being flown by 2nd Lieutenant Raymond Paaske.

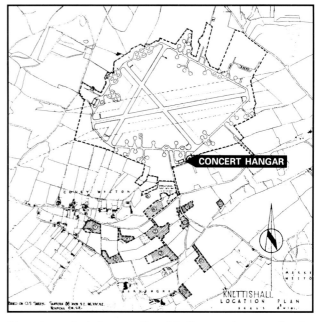

After the end of the war, Knettishall was taken over by the Royal Air Force, being finally closed down in 1957. The site of the concert hangar, which lay beside the technical site on the southern perimeter, is now just a few yards to the east of the road between Knettishall and Coney Weston which now crosses the airfield.

Langford Lodge Station 597

CO. ANTRIM, NORTHERN IRELAND

The airfield at Langford Lodge, 15 miles outside Belfast, beside Lough Neagh in County Antrim, Northern Ireland, was opened in 1942, being taken over by the VIII Air Force Service Command and used as Base Air Depot No. 3.

During the afternoon of Sunday, August 13, 1944, Captain Glenn Miller and the dance band combo from the American Band of the AEF landed at Langford Lodge in two C-47 transport planes after a 1½-hour flight from Twinwood Farm. After arrival at the large air base depot, they were collected by truck and taken first to the American Red Cross Club in Belfast (see page 31). They then returned to Langford Lodge during the early evening and, after a meal, they gave a second concert for officers and enlisted personnel in the cinema-cum-theatre.

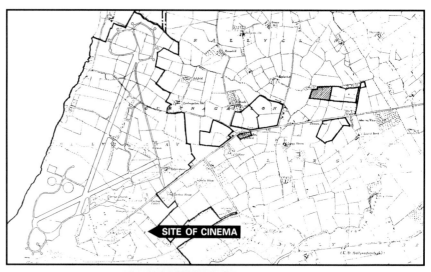

SITE OF CINEMA

Left: **Glenn, here still a Captain, directs the band in the cinema at Langford Lodge airfield, which was situated on Site No. 6, near the Station Headquarters. The cinema was known as the Project Magnet Hall, or Pro-Ma Hall for short, and is referred to as such in the airfield records which state that the concert lasted from 1930 to 2145 hours and that the crowd was 750 strong — about the maximum the two-storey building could hold. The picture *(above)* of Glenn at the top of a fire escape (note the 'panic bars' on the door) was therefore probably taken by the first floor fire exit. Knocked down many years ago when the aerodrome was owned by the Martin Baker company (of ejector seat fame), the cinema site is now derelict, being pictured for us *(below)* by local historian, John Quinn, seen standing where the entrance once lay. The same doorway is visible behind Glenn in the 1944 shot. Now vacated by Martin Baker, the airfield is accessible to visitors, Site No. 3 being the home of the Station 597 Wartime Centre Museum.**

De Montfort Hall

LEICESTER

Leicester's concert hall pictured under floodlights in 1933. During the 1960s, the De Montfort Hall was popularised when it was used for Saturday afternoon wrestling compèred by Kent Walton and broadcast by the ITV television network. Today, it is still in use as a concert hall.

On the evening of Monday, September 11, 1944, Glenn Miller and the American Band of the AEF gave a 90-minute concert for the US 82nd Airborne Division at the De Montfort Hall in Leicester. It was to be the last entertainment for the paratroopers about to take part in Operation 'Market Garden' (the airborne drop on Holland) the following Sunday. Miller and the band were introduced to the officers and enlisted men packed into the hall by the Assistant Division Commander, General James M. Gavin.

In view of the fact that the men were in isolation pending the forthcoming operation, news of the concert was kept extremely quiet and no mention was ever made of it in the local Leicester newspapers. Also no photos appear to have been taken.

The Glenn Miller (UK) Orchestra, conducted by John Watson, performed a special concert in the hall on November 17, 1995.

The song for which Glenn Miller is most closely associated, and which opened virtually every concert in Britain, was written by him and first published by the Robbins Music Corporation of New York in 1939. Although primarily played as an instrumental, Mitchell Parish set it to words:

I stand at your gate and the song that I sing is of moonlight,
I stand and I wait for the touch of your hand in the June night,
The roses are sighing a Moonlight Serenade,
The stars are aglow and tonight how their light sets me dreaming,

My love, do you know that your eyes are like stars brightly beaming?
I bring you and sing you a Moonlight Serenade.
Let us stray till break of day in love's 'valley of dreams',
Just you and I, a summer sky,
a heavenly breeze kissing the trees,
So don't let me wait,
come to me tenderly in the June night,
I stand at your gate and I sing you a song in the moonlight,
A love song, my darling, a Moonlight Serenade.

London

Due to the flying bomb campaign, the American Band of the AEF was billeted in London for only three days (from Thursday, June 29, to Sunday, July 2) at 25 Sloane Court, Chelsea, before Miller had them moved out to Bedford. Nevertheless, they were to see quite a lot more of the city in the months ahead.

The orchestra's first broadcast from the capital was on July 27 from the American Red Cross Club — better known as Rainbow Corner — in Shaftesbury Avenue. Later that same day, they gave their first public concert at the Plaza in Lower Regent Street. Three days later, on Sunday, July 30, Captain Miller and the band were the invited guests on the BBC's *Variety Bandbox* programme, recorded at the Queensbury All Services Club in Old Compton Street.

They were again in London on Thursday, August 10, when the Swing Shift (the dance band minus the string section) played again at Rainbow Corner. The full orchestra also broadcast later that evening from the Paris Cinema in Lower Regent Street in their own series *The American Band of the AEF* with British guest star, Paula Green.

The next time they were in London as a complete unit was on Thursday, August 31, although the relief pianist, Jack Russin, was at the Queensbury All Services Club with the visiting American star, Bing Crosby, on Sunday, August 27.

From September 14, Glenn Miller and the American Band of the AEF performed weekly at the Queensbury All Services Club.

Piccadilly Circus during the war looking up Shaftesbury Avenue. The statue of Eros was removed during the war years to prevent possible damage from air raids.

Glenn spent quite a lot of time in London during his time in Britain, staying at his suite in the Mount Royal Hotel (see page 69) during the autumn.

Left: In Piccadilly Circus on Friday, September 29, 1944, Don Haynes, the band's Executive Officer, points out the wartime location of Rainbow Corner in Shaftesbury Avenue (see page

70) to Corporal Murray Kane, one of The Crew Chiefs singing group. *Right:* Author Chris Way (left) and *After the Battle* editor, Winston Ramsey recreate the scene fifty years later.

Major Miller with Colonel Ed Kirby, two unidentified civilians (front row), Sergeant Vick Knight, Dinah Shore, and Sergeant Dick Dudley pictured outside No. 41 Berkeley Square (actually

in Hill Street) on the afternoon of Saturday, September 16, 1944. They had most probably just visited the Economic Warfare division of the American Embassy at No. 40.

25 Sloane Court

CHELSEA

Above: No. 25 Sloane Court after the V1 blast on July 3, 1944. This was the second most serious V1 incident, causing the most deaths to military personnel — 64 in all — plus 50 injured and 10 civilians killed. *Below:* Royal Hospital Road is behind the photographer in our comparison view, taken looking down Sloane Court East.

On Thursday, June 29, 1944, the musicians of the Glenn Miller Army Air Forces Band arrived at Euston Station in London, after an overnight train journey from Gourock in Scotland. This was at the height of the V1 flying bomb attack on the capital and they arrived to be greeted by an air raid alert.

The band made their way to their billets at 25 Sloane Court, Chelsea, but, situated in the middle of what was known as 'Buzz-Bomb Alley' (due to the large numbers of flying bombs going over this part of London), Captain Miller was far from happy with this situation. He had not spent months building up his band of 60 musicians just to have it blown to pieces and lose everything with one chance V1 blast. Together with 2nd Lieutenant Don Haynes, his Executive Officer, he therefore drove out to Supreme Headquarters located in Bushy Park, Teddington, (see page 117) to arrange for alternative accommodation to be made available outside London.

On the first night, the late Johnny Desmond recalled several members of the band going up to the roof to watch the 'buzz-bombs' coming over. It looked a very serious situation and many of the musicians became somewhat anxious to find themselves suddenly living in a city under fire.

However, as it turned out, they were only at Sloane Court for three nights, the transfer to Bedford being made on Sunday morning, July 2. It was a fortuitous move, for by Tuesday morning 25 Sloane Court was a shambles after a V1 exploded in the road in front of the building. Don Haynes and his driver heard later that 25 MPs had been killed, plus 70 *(sic)* others including some WACs. The orchestra had only just got out in the nick of time!

Mount Royal Hotel

BRYANSTON STREET

The Mount Royal, seen here in 1933, was one of over 15 West End hotels used by American forces during the war for officers' duty billets in London. Although it fronts Oxford Street, the entrance is round the back in Bryanston Street. Today, the former Harry's Bar on the first floor has been turned into the Glenn Miller Bar *(below right)* where there is an appropriate display of photographs, records, sleeves and sheet music. Glenn's recordings are played throughout opening hours.

When Glenn Miller arrived in London in late June 1944, he and Paul Dudley, his radio producer, were allocated a suite of rooms at the Mount Royal Hotel in Bryanston Street, just off Marble Arch. Glenn's was situated on the first floor (US second floor, as Americans treat the ground floor as the first), together with another for Don Haynes. This accommodation was retained throughout their stay in England.

From December 12 until the afternoon of December 14 Miller waited at the Mount Royal Hotel for the weather to improve so he could travel to Bovingdon and board the SHAEF 'shuttle' plane for France. The weather did not improve and all flights were cancelled. It was at the Mount Royal that Glenn, by now desperate for a place on a flight to Paris, spoke on the telephone with Don Haynes during which the arrangements were made for an alternative flight from Twinwood Farm the following day (see page 129). Producer Cecil Madden, the last person from the BBC to talk to Glenn before his death, visited the Mount Royal on December 13 for a meeting with Miller.

The little-altered hotel exterior in 1995 with Littlewoods at street level.

Of more than a dozen American Red Cross Clubs in London in 1944, the one located in Shaftesbury Avenue, on the corner of Windmill Street, was undoubtedly the most famous. It became known as Rainbow Corner from the rainbow shoulder flash worn by the staff at the club. The radio broadcasts came from 'Dunker's Den' situated in the basement, the name coined from the American habit of dipping doughnuts in their coffee. The club itself had been opened four years earlier in the autumn of 1940 to provide the volunteer American pilots of the famed Eagle Squadron a place in London offering relaxation and entertainment, but it came into its own after US forces arrived in Britain en masse.

American Red Cross Club

RAINBOW CORNER, SHAFTESBURY AVENUE

On the afternoon of Thursday, July 27, 1944, Glenn Miller and the dance band unit from the American Band of the Supreme Allied Command, with drummer Sergeant Ray McKinley, were invited by BBC producer Cecil Madden to be the musical guests on his *American Eagle in Britain* programme to be broadcast from the American Red Cross Club, run by Fred Astaire's sister Adele, located on the corner of Windmill Street and Shaftesbury Avenue. Glenn jumped at the chance to record the broadcast because it was to be relayed coast-to-coast in the USA. It was also a way of both Miller and the band giving the folks back home greetings from war-torn London, without infringing too much on the wartime censorship regulations.

The first broadcast from Rainbow Corner was such a success that Glenn and the band were invited back again on four more occasions: August 10, August 31, September 14, and September 28. Perhaps the most evocative performance of these was the one held on the afternoon of Thursday, August 31, when British composer Michael Carr and American film star and dancer Fred Astaire were guests, and Fred danced to a trio which included Sergeants Ray McKinley (drums), Mel Powell (piano) and Michael 'Peanuts' Hucko (clarinet).

Fred Astaire, BBC producer Cecil Madden, and Adele Astaire, during the *American Eagle in Britain* programme which was broadcast from 'Dunker's Den' at the American Red Cross Club on August 31, 1944.

Above: **A view of the foyer which gives a good idea of the atmosphere within the club in 1944.** Below: **The whole block has since been demolished for office and shop redevelopment.** The comparison was taken from a window of the Golden Nugget Casino on the opposite side of Shaftesbury Avenue by special arrangement with London Clubs International.

Plaza Cinema

LOWER REGENT STREET

Captain Glenn Miller directs the American Band of the Supreme Allied Command as the singing group The Crew Chiefs, plus trumpeter Sergeant Bobby Nichols, perform _Juke-box Saturday Night_ at the Plaza cinema on Thursday, July 27, 1944.

After their appearance at the Rainbow Corner American Red Cross Club on the afternoon of Thursday, July 27, Glenn Miller and the band made their first public appearance in Britain at a special charity concert held to mark the opening of the London Stage Door Canteen at 201 Piccadilly on August 31. This special concert preceded the premiere of the new Bing Crosby film _Going My Way_ at the Plaza in Lower Regent Street. The cinema was packed not only with members of the public but all the top British musicians. News of Glenn's presence had travelled fast, and all wanted to see and hear this great orchestra perform — and what a performance it was! The concert raised £4,000 for the new Canteen.

PROGRAMME

1.

The American Band
Of The Supreme Command
Conducted by

CAPT. GLENN MILLER

2.

PARAMOUNT PRESENTE
"Going my way"

STARRING

BING CROSBY

BARRY FITZGERALD   JAMES BROWN

FRANK McHUGH   JEAN HEATHER

GENE LOCKHART   PORTER HALL

FORTUNIO BONANOVA

and

RISË STEVENS

Famous Contralto of Metropolitan Opera Association

Screen Play by Frank Butler and Frank Cavett

Produced and Directed by Leo McCarey

A PARAMOUNT PICTURE

THE LONDON STAGE DOOR CANTEEN

The London Stage Door Canteen at 201, Piccadilly, will be unique in presenting every evening a Stage Show generously given by prominent members of the Stage, Screen and Radio. There will also be dancing, and light refreshments will be provided at nominal prices.

All non-commissioned ranks—men and women—of the Armed Forces of the British Empire, United States of America, and other Allied Nations will be welcomed every day from 5 p.m. to 11 p.m. Up to 1,000 people can be accommodated.

Surely, no cause can have a greater appeal than to bring friendship and give happiness to the men and women of the Services when they come to London on leave, or return from the Battle front.

FILM PREMIERE

President :
H.R.H. THE DUKE OF GLOUCESTER,
K.G., K.T., K.P., P.C., G.M.B., G.C.M.G., G.C.V.O.

Vice-Presidents :
HIS EXCELLENCY THE HON. JOHN G. WINANT AND MRS. WINANT.
MRS. WINSTON CHURCHILL.

Chairman :
THE HON. LADY FOX.

Patrons :
RT. HON. VISCOUNT AND VISCOUNTESS CRANBORNE.
VISCOUNT NUFFIELD, G.B.E., D.L.
LORD AND LADY McGOWAN.
RT. HON. ANTHONY EDEN, M.C., M.P., AND MRS. EDEN.
COL. THE RT. HON. OLIVER STANLEY, M.C., M.P.
RT. HON. A. V. ALEXANDER, C.H., M.P., AND MRS. ALEXANDER.
RT. HON. SIR ARCHIBALD SINCLAIR, K.T., C.M.G., M.P., AND LADY SINCLAIR
LADY PEEL.
AIR COMMODORE F. BEAUMONT.
MRS. CHARLES DICKSON.
MISS DOROTHY DICKSON.
MR. ALFRED LUNT.
MRS. LEONARD PLUGGE.
MR. J. ARTHUR RANK.

Organiser : JOHN J. DAVIES

> THE CHAIRMAN, THE HON. LADY FOX, WISHES TO EXPRESS MOST GRATEFUL THANKS TO ALL THOSE WHO HAVE SO GENEROUSLY HELPED TO MAKE THIS PREMIERE A SUCCESS.

Above left: **In the foyer of the Plaza (L-R): J. Arthur Rank, Alfred Lunt, Jack Harding, Lady Fox, Mrs Anthony Eden, Dorothy Dickson, Captain Glenn Miller, 2nd Lieutenant Don Haynes and Sergeant Paul Dudley (promoted to Warrant Officer on August 19 to enable him to attend meetings in Officers' Messes with Miller and Haynes).** *Left and above:* **Like most cinemas, the Plaza is now a multi-screen theatre.**

Stage Door Canteen

PICCADILLY

Bing Crosby sings for the Allied audience *(above)* accompanied on piano by Pfc Jack Russin of Glenn's band, at the opening of the London Stage Door Canteen. The auditorium was located on the first (US second) floor, now occupied by Trans World Airways for their London booking office *(below)*.

Having performed at the charity performance in the Plaza cinema on Thursday, July 27, the American Band of the AEF had provided £4,000 for the opening of the London Stage Door Canteen. Rather surprisingly, Glenn and the band never actually performed there although pianist Pfc Jack Russin accompanied Bing Crosby at the opening on the evening of August 31.

The London Stage Door Canteen was located at No. 201 Piccadilly, and it became a meeting place for any Allied serviceman or woman seeking to be entertained by some of the top singing stars and personalities of the day. No ticket was required, the only condition for entry was to be in uniform. The idea came from the USA and the club was run by Dorothy Dickson and Mrs Anthony

Eden. Anthony Eden, Britain's debonair Foreign Secretary, opened the Canteen on the same evening that Bing Crosby, Jack Russin and Fred Astaire appeared. Also on hand was the RAF Dance Orchestra (the Squadronaires) directed by Sergeant Jimmy Miller. Many more top British and American stars would perform in this famous venue during the one year of its existence.

The Stage Door Canteen was opened by the Secretary of State for Foreign Affairs, Anthony Eden, who commented that 'Miss Dorothy Dickson and her friends are doing more for the friendly relations of countries than all the Foreign Offices and State Departments do by driving their quills, from one year's end to another'. This was the scene outside on Thursday, August 31, as Mr Eden arrived with his wife.

The changing face of the Stage Door Canteen. TWA have always been closely involved with the building, this picture dating from 1949 when the BBC still used part of the basement for a studio.

Over the years, aviation has also changed, being reflected in the shopfront, seen as it was *(left)* in 1952 and *(right)* in 1960.

Below: Boots the Chemist now occupy the ground floor and the basement where the artistes' dressing rooms were located.

American Broadcasting Station in Europe

Major Glenn Miller broadcasting with Irene Manning, wearing USO uniform, for the ABSIE *Wehrmacht Hour* series on the affternoon of Wednesday, December 6, 1944.

The American Forces Network (AFN) started life at 5.45 p.m. on Sunday, July 4, 1943, broadcasting from their very cramped studios at 11 Carlos Place. However, with the build up for the invasion of Europe, the BBC loaned out several larger studios in London to the American forces and AFN moved into 80 Portland Place during May 1944.

The previous month, it had been announced that the American Broadcasting Station in Europe (ABSIE as it became known) would go on the air on Sunday, April 30 as an auxiliary to the BBC. Its head office was located in Soho at 2 Sheraton Street with its operational base just a few yards away in Film House, just around the corner in Wardour Street. As part of the US Office of War Information (OWI), ABSIE broadcast propaganda shows to occupied Europe and also to German troops in an anti-'Lord Haw Haw' rôle.

The studios of AFN were transferred to Germany in 1945. Their London office — No. 80 Portland Place (on the left) — was taken over by the Chartered Institute of Transport in December 1947 and, ten years later, Nos. 76 and 78 were demolished and redeveloped for the City and Guilds of London Institute.

Left: This picture was taken in 1955, before the wartime aspect of the buildings changed. *Right:* Forty years on, when we took this comparison in October 1995, the City and Guilds building was once again being gutted and refurbished for the Institute of Physics.

The late Don Haynes wrote in his diary during the autumn of 1944 that the band would record special German propaganda shows and that either he, Paul Dudley, or Glenn, would then take them to a small basement studio in London for broadcast. This refers to the *Wehrmacht Hour* recordings made by the orchestra at the Abbey Road Studios (see page 78). The small basement studio referred to was the ABSIE set up in Wardour Street.

Today, technology has moved on apace, and the basement studios in Film House have since been completely reconstructed and are now used by TVI Limited — a post-production video editing organisation. This is the Control Machine Room from where live playouts of TV programmes are made.

The recordings made on Monday, November 13 featured American film star and singer Irene Manning who was on a USO tour of Europe at the time. The four recordings made that day at Abbey Road were not able to have the introductions put on at the same time because Glenn had flown to Paris the same day. However, when the programmes were broadcast by ABSIE on Wednesday, December 6, both Glenn Miller and Irene Manning added live introductions direct from the ABSIE studios.

An announcement was made on the BBC news at 6 p.m. on April 26, 1944 that ABSIE — the American Broadcasting Station in Europe — would start transmissions the following Sunday.

Left: **Its studios were located in the basement of No. 142 Wardour Street with its head office in No. 2 Sheraton Street (on the far left).** *Right:* **Today, the entrance looks little altered.**

Abbey Road Studios

ST JOHN'S WOOD

Major Miller conducts the band in Studio No. 1 on September 16, 1944. The recordings made that day were released in 1995 by *Conifer Happy Days* on tape and compact disc and are now available as *Glenn Miller — The Lost Recordings*.

During the afternoon of Saturday, September 16, Major Glenn Miller and the American Band of the AEF, with special guest, singer Dinah Shore, made a set of special recordings in Studio No. 1 at the HMV Abbey Road studios in St John's Wood. The recordings, which were intended for Service charities, were produced during a four-hour session. Studio No. 1 is huge, with excellent acoustics, and no better location could have been found to record the whole 60-piece Miller AEF orchestra. As it turned out, it was to be over 50 years before the four titles recorded that day for the charity release would be issued. Also reputedly recorded at the same session was the sound track for a film but no trace of that has ever been found.

Miller and the American Band of the AEF made further recordings at the Abbey Road studios during October and November for the American Broadcasting Station in Europe, better known as ABSIE (see page 76). The first session began at 2 p.m. on Monday, October 30 and lasted four hours. The recordings were for ABSIE's propaganda series *Wehrmacht Hour* which was transmitted weekly to occupied Europe. On these recordings, Glenn was joined by the programme's co-host, Ilse Weinberger, a German announcer who worked for the US Office of War Information. During the series, Ilse taught Miller to speak some basic German. The performances were recorded onto masters, then turned into 12-inch, 78rpm

Glenn conducting the saxophones and trombones during the same session.

On September 16, 1994, exactly 50 years later, author Chris Way stands on the same spot in the studios in Abbey Road which are now part of the EMI organisation.

Major Glenn Miller with singer Dinah Shore pictured at the HMV Studios in Abbey Road on the afternoon of Saturday, September 16, 1944.

records which were then taken over to the ABSIE studios for transmission every Wednesday at 2 p.m.

Altogether, Glenn and the band held four recording sessions at Abbey Road, each on a Monday: on October 30, November 6, November 20, and November 27. They also produced nine ABSIE shows to be broadcast in the afternoons of November 8, 15, 22, 29, and December 6, 13, 20, and 27 (all Wednesdays), plus one other which was to go out on

Wednesday, January 3, 1945. However, the last two were never transmitted due to the untimely death of Miller on December 15, and the subsequent announcement of his disappearance by the BBC on Christmas Eve.

The series featured American guest singer and film star, Irene Manning, who was on a USO tour in the autumn of 1944. Irene, who, like Sergeant Johnny Desmond, could sing in German, was famous for her appearance in the James Cagney film *Yankee Doodle*

Dandy, and she recorded four tracks with Glenn at Abbey Road in November 1944. All four were used in programme number five, broadcast on December 6.

Major Glenn Miller, 2nd Lieutenant Don Haynes and Warrant Officer Paul Dudley, recorded special Christmas messages at Abbey Road on the morning of December 6 for their wives back home. Glenn's was sent to the USA but by the time his wife Helen played it, he had already gone missing.

Glenn checks through his script with Ilse Weinberger at the ABSIE microphone at Abbey Road on October 30.

The same studios were to achieve everlasting fame some 25 years later when the Beatles recorded their *Abbey Road* album here, being photographed for the cover on this zebra crossing. The studio is behind the low white wall on the left.

Paris Cinema

LOWER REGENT STREET

The interior of the cinema as it appeared in November 1946.

Glenn Miller and his band made four broadcasts from the studio at the BBC Paris Cinema Radio Theatre located in Lower Regent Street. The first was on Thursday, August 10, when British singing star Paula Green from the Geraldo Orchestra was the guest singer on the *American Band of the AEF* programme when she sang the Dinah Shore hit *Tessa's Torch Song* from the Hollywood feature film *Up in Arms*. Directly afterwards, Miller and the orchestra recorded a special broadcast at the theatre called the *NBA Convention Salute* for the National Broadcasters Association. This featured, besides others, Colonel Ed Kirby and Sergeant Broderick Crawford, and was recorded between 9.15 and 11 p.m. Both the live broadcast and the recordings were attended by an audience of around two hundred.

The third broadcast from this venue was undoubtedly the most famous, as it featured Bing Crosby during his first visit to England. Bing teamed up with the band on Thursday, August 31, and the event turned out to be one of the highlights of the year in London.

The fourth broadcast from the Paris Cinema by Glenn and the band came during the recording of the regular BBC *Atlantic Spotlight* programme that was re-broadcast across the USA the following week and also by the BBC as a joint link-up. Also starring from the USA were Glenn's old gang from his civilian bandleader days, Marion Hutton and Paula Kelly and the Modernaires vocal group. Marion Hutton sang from Atlantic City while Miller conducted the orchestra and The Crew Chiefs held forth with Glenn's 1942 hit, *Jukebox Saturday Night*. This recording took place on Saturday, September 2.

Bing Crosby with Glenn Miller in the Grosvenor House Hotel on August 31 immediately before going to the Paris Cinema for the live broadcast.

After the war, the Paris Cinema in Lower Regent Street was regularly used by the BBC and many programmes have been broadcast from, or recorded in, this theatre. It was closed early in 1995, the last broadcast going out on February 26.

The Stoll Theatre was conceived by the American impressario Oscar Hammerstein as a rival to the Royal Opera House in Covent Garden and it opened as the London Opera House in 1911. However, it was not a success and it was taken over by

Oswald Stoll in 1916. It was initially converted into a cinema — the Stoll Picture Theatre — the following year, later reverting to the Stoll Theatre. It closed in 1957 and an office block incorporating the Royalty Theatre now stands on the site.

Stoll Theatre

KINGSWAY

On Sunday, October 15, 1944, the sixth annual Jazz Jamboree was held at the Stoll Theatre in Kingsway. This charity event by all the top British bands continued even during the war, all the proceeds going to the British Musicians' Union. The arranger for the bands participating in the 1944 event was British trombonist, Ted Heath. Ted had asked Miller if the American Band of the AEF could take part, thus hoping to make the 1944 Jamboree the best ever, and Glenn promised to do what he could. However, on the appointed day, Heath had nearly given up all hope as band after band performed their piece with no sign of the appearance of Miller. 'Then, suddenly, down Kingsway came all these American trucks', recalled Ted. 'Glenn Miller had brought the entire orchestra, including music stands — everything'. As it turned out, the Glenn Miller band were the biggest ever hit.

This was the second and last appearance of the band before a paying audience, and perhaps its most successful. The band played all the popular items before Sergeant Johnny Desmond was brought on to sing the wartime romantic ballads, backed by the lush Norman Leyden arrangements featuring the string section with the unique 'Miller Sound'. Ten-year-old boy wonder drummer, Victor Feldman, joined the quartet for a swinging rendition of *Sweet Georgia Brown*, much to the delight of Miller himself. Glenn's programme at the Jazz Jamboree lasted 30 minutes; afterwards he was invited to the Feldman Swing Club in Oxford Street.

Above right: **This 1941 shot of people lined up for a 'Sword of the Spirit' meeting, hosted by Cardinal Hinsley, gives a good atmospheric feel to queueing in wartime at the Stoll, since swept away by a faceless redevelopment** *(right).*

THE MUSICIANS' SOCIAL AND BENEVOLENT COUNCIL

HAS PLEASURE IN PRESENTING

"JAZZ JAMBOREE, 1944"

Dedicated to ALFRED H. MORGAN, the Council's retiring Hon. Acting Secretary

STOLL THEATRE, KINGSWAY

SUNDAY, OCTOBER 15th, 1944

ACKNOWLEDGMENTS

The Council desire to express their gratitude to :—

The Stoll Picture Theatre (Kingsway), Ltd., and Staff for their cordial co-operation.

The B.B.C. for broadcasting twenty-five minutes in the General Forces Programme.

Tommy Trinder, for his co-operation and invaluable services as Compere.

Every Band Leader, Vocalist, and Instrumentalist appearing in the Bill.

The Entrants, Judges, Geraldo's Orchestra, The Dance Orchestra of H.M. Royal Air Force, and all who have ...

Every ... who ... their services, for the service to the length of ... who ... be ...

All the Advertisers in the Programme ...

All the Volunteers at the Front and Back of the House; the Stewards, Programme Sellers, and others.

Mr. Leon Goodman of Leon Goodman Displays, Ltd., for designing the original Programme cover.

Messrs. Boosey & Hawkes for their kindness in supplying us with Basses for use at this Concert.

Messrs. Chappell & Co., Ltd., for supplying their excellent Grand Pianos.

The Premier Drum Co., Ltd., for supplying all Drum Outfits for use at this Concert.

The Melody Maker and General Press for the help they have given.

The London District Committee of the Musicians' Union for permitting its members to appear gratuitously.

The Performing Right Society has granted free permission for the use of its repertoire on this occasion and the Council desire to thank the composers and owners of the copyright in the music performed for their generosity in forgoing the fees to which they are entitled.

THE MUSICIANS' SOCIAL AND BENEVOLENT COUNCIL

5 Egmont House

116 Shaftesbury Avenue, London, W.1

Telephone : GERrard 2096

This Programme is printed in accordance with Wartime Regulations

Price ONE SHILLING

PROGRAMME

Compere TOMMY TRINDER

THE LONDON COLISEUM ORCHESTRA
Under the Direction of REGINALD BURSTON

Violins :	JOE DEMBINA (Leader)	Cellos :	J. BRADY
	M. JEKEL		J. SIGALL
	S. WALLER		G. REGAN
	C. M. KEMP	Trumpets:	G. MORGAN
	J. PALMER	Piano :	F. BRETON
	E. W. ANDERSON	Trombones:	D. CARTER
	W. PENMAN		E. SOWDEN
	H. CHEVERIN	Harp :	MAY SALKELD
Violas :	L. MEER	Drums & Tymps. :	WAG. ABBEY
	F. CRAMER	Flute & Piccolo :	R. E. CROSS
Clarinets :	A. BUTTEN	Bass :	W. MACDONALD
	J. CLEVERLEY		

LOU PREAGER AND HIS ORCHESTRA

1st Trumpet :	A. "TICH" CHARLTON	3rd Tenor Sax :	DENNIS CRACKNELL
2nd Trumpet :	HARRY FINCH	Baritone Sax :	FRED CRANSTONE
3rd Trumpet :	KEN EXTON	Guitar :	PAUL RICH
1st Alto & Clar. :	JACK CARTER	Bass :	DOUG. CALDERWOOD
2nd Alto :	DON PEARSALL	Drums :	NORRIS GRUNDY
1st Tenor Sax :	JOHNNIE GRAY	Piano :	BILLY PENROSE
2nd Tenor Sax :	NORMAN BURGESS	Vocaliste :	EDNA KAYE

FRANK DENIZ "SPIRITS OF RHYTHM "
(By arrangement with Eric Winstone)

Piano :	CLARE DENIZ	Electric Guitar :	FRANK DENIZ
Tenor Sax :	J. SKIDMORE	Bass :	T. WADMORE
Drums :	T. BUTLIN		

No. 1 BALLOON CENTRE DANCE ORCHESTRA
A Band of H.M. Royal Air Force
(By kind permission of the Officer Commanding)
Directed by PAUL FENOULHET

1st Trumpet :	CHICK SMITH	1st Tenor Sax :	CLIFF TIMMS
2nd Trumpet :	LES LAMBERT	2nd Tenor Sax :	BASIL SKINNER
3rd Trumpet :	TED ALLABY	Piano :	PAT DODD
1st Trombone :	HARRY ROCHE	Guitar :	JOE YOUNG
2nd Trombone :	JOE CORDELL	Bass :	JOCK REID
1st Alto Sax :	IZZY DUMAN	Drums :	GEORGE FIERSTONE
2nd Alto Sax :	BILL APPS	Vocalist :	DENNY DENNIS

THE FELDMAN TRIO

Clar. : ROBERT FELDMAN.   Piano-Acc. : MONTY FELDMAN.   Drums : VICTOR FELDMAN.

TED HEATH AND HIS MUSIC

Saxophones :	LESLIE GILBERT	Trombones :	TED HEATH
	MICHAEL KREIN		WOOLF PHILLIPS
	DEREK HAWKINS		LES CAREW
	AUBREY FRANKS		GEORGE ROWE
	NORMAN IMPEY	Drums :	JACK PARNELL
Trumpets :	MAX GOLDBERG	Piano :	RONNIE SELBY
	ARTHUR MOUNCEY	Guitar :	FREDDY PHILLIPS
	CLIFF HAINES	Bass :	GEORGE GARNETT
	RONNIE PRIEST		

ROBERTO INGLEZ AND HIS RUMBA BAND

Piano :	ROBERTO INGLEZ	Bass :	BILL WILDER
Bongoes :	BILLY DUFFY	Claves :	JAMES CUMMINGS
Guitar :	SID BISSETT	Maraccas :	LOUIS ORTIZ
Trumpet :	ANDREW COOK	Guiro :	DONALDO GRIFFITHS

"JAZZ JAMBOREE AWARD "
(A Competition for the Best Original Jazz Composition)
The Three Selected Entries for Final Judging

Judges : STANLEY BLACK, STANLEY BOWSHER, GEORGE EVANS, T/Sgt. JERRY GRAY, and HARRY SARTON

Played by THE DANCE ORCHESTRA OF H.M. ROYAL AIR FORCE

FRANK WEIR AND HIS ORCHESTRA

Trumpets :	KENNY BAKER	Violins :	REG LEOPOLD
	ALFIE NOAKES		SID SAX
	TOMMY ANDERSON		CHARLES KATZ
Trombones :	LAD BUSBY		BILLY MILLER
	HARRY ROCHE	Violas :	CYRIL STAPLETON
	JIMMY COOMBS		MAURICE LOBAN
Saxophones :	CLIFF TOWNSHEND		DAVID BELLMAN
	HARRY SMITH	'Cellos :	MAURICE WESTERBY
	HARRY LEWIS		GEORGE ROTH
	FREDDY GARDNER	Drums :	NORMAN BURNS
	FRED BALLERINI	Bass :	DON STUTELY
		Guitar :	SID JACOBSON
		Piano :	GEORGE SHEARING

GERALDO AND HIS ORCHESTRA

1st Trumpet :	ALFIE NOAKES	1st Tenor Sax :	BILLY AMSTELL
2nd Trumpet :	TIM CASEY	2nd Tenor Sax :	GEORGE HARRIS
3rd Trumpet :	CHICK SMITH	Baritone Sax :	PHIL GOODY
1st Trombone :	TED HEATH	Piano :	SIDNEY BRIGHT
2nd Trombone :	ERIC TANN	Drums :	MAURICE BURMAN
3rd Trombone :	JOE FERRIE	Guitar :	IVOR MAIRANTS
1st Alto Sax :	DOUGIE ROBINSON	Bass :	JACK COLLIER
2nd Alto Sax :	WALLY STOTT	Vocalists :	LEN CAMBER
			JOHNNY GREEN

PHIL GREEN AND HIS DIXIELAND BAND

Trumpet :	DUNCAN WHYTE	Drums :	JOHNNY MARKS
Trombone :	JOCK BAIN	Bass :	MAURICE REID
Clarinet :	DAVE GREEN	Guitar :	DENNIS WRIGHT
Tenor Sax :	ARTY WILLIAMS	Piano :	MARION LOTHIAN

THE DANCE ORCHESTRA OF H.M. ROYAL AIR FORCE
(By kind permission of the Air Council)

Vocalist (Cond'or) :	Sgt. JIMMY MILLER	Saxophones :	L.A.C. TOMMY BRADBURY
Trumpets :	Cpl. TOMMY McQUATER		L.A.C. MONTY LESTER
	L.A.C. ARCHIE CRAIG		L.A.C. ANDY McDEVITT
	L.A.C. KENNY BAKER		L.A.C. JIMMY DURRANT
Trombones :	L.A.C. ERIC BREEZE	Guitar :	L.A.C. SID COLIN
	L.A.C. GEORGE CHISHOLM	Bass :	L.A.C. ARTHUR MADEN
Piano :	L.A.C. RONNIE ALDRICH	Drums :	L.A.C. JOCK CUMMINGS

VIC LEWIS–JACK PARNELL AND THEIR JAZZMEN

Guitar :	VIC LEWIS	Clarinet :	CLIFF TOWNSHEND
Drums :	JACK PARNELL	Piano :	DICK KATZ
Trumpet :	BILLY RIDDICK	Bass :	BERT HOWARD
Sop. & Alto Sax :	RONNY CHAMBERLAIN		

ALL-STAR BAND ("MELODY MAKER" POLL 1944)

Trumpets :	KENNY BAKER	Alto Saxes :	HARRY HAYES
	TOMMY McQUATER		DOUGIE ROBINSON
	CHICK SMITH	Tenor Saxes :	AUBREY FRANKS
	ARTHUR MOUNCEY		BUDDY FEATHERSTONHAUGH
Trombones :	GEORGE CHISHOLM (Leader)	Baritone Sax :	JIMMY DURRANT
	WOOLF PHILLIPS	Piano :	GEORGE SHEARING
	ERIC BREEZE	Drums :	JACK PARNELL
	DON MACAFFER	Guitar :	IVOR MAIRANTS
		Bass :	TOMMY BROMLEY

THE AMERICAN BAND OF THE A.E.F.
Conducted by MAJOR GLENN MILLER

Executive Officer :	Lt. DON W. HAYNES	Director of Programmes :	W.O. PAUL DUDLEY
Piano :	S/Sgt. MEL POWELL	French Horn :	Cpl. ADDISON COLLINS, Jr.
Drums :	Cpl. JACK RUSIN	Violins :	S/Sgt. GEORGE OCKNER
	T/Sgt. RAY McKINLEY		S/Sgt. HARRY KATZMAN
	Cpl. FRANK IPPOLITO		Cpl. ERNEST KARDOS
Guitar :	Sgt. CARMEN MASTREN		Cpl. EUGENE BERGEN
Bass :	S/Sgt. TRIGGER ALPERT		S/Sgt. CARL SWANSON
	Cpl. JOE SHULMAN		Cpl. MILTON EDELSON
Trumpets :	M/Sgt. ZEKE ZARCHY		Sgt. DAVE HERMAN
	Sgt. BOB NICHOLS		Cpl. PHIL COGLIANO
	Sgt. WHITEY THOMAS		Cpl. JOSEPH KOWALEWSKI
	Cpl. BERNIE PRIVEN		Sgt. DAVE SCHWARTZ
	Cpl. JACK STEELE		Cpl. HENRY BRYNAN
Trombones :	Sgt. JIMMY PRIDDY		Cpl. EARL CORNWELL
	Cpl. JOHN HALLIBURTON		P.F.C. FRED. OSTROVSKY
	Cpl. LARRY HALL		Cpl. MORRIS BIALKIN
	P.F.C. NAT PECK		Cpl. BOB RIPLEY
Vocalist :	Sgt. JOHNNIE DESMOND		Sgt. STANLEY HARRIS
Crew Chiefs :	Cpl. STEVE STECK		Cpl. EMANUEL WISHNOW
	Cpl. EUGENE STECK		Cpl. DAVE SACKSON
	Cpl. ARTHUR MALVIN		Cpl. NATE KAPROFF
	Cpl. MURRAY KANE		Cpl. RICHARD MOTOLINSKI
	Cpl. LYNN ALLISON		
Saxophones :	S/Sgt. HANK FREEMAN	Arrangers :	T/Sgt. JERRY GRAY
	Sgt. MICHAEL HUCKO		M/Sgt. NORM LAYDEN
	Sgt. VINCE CARBONE		S/Sgt. RALPH WILKINSON
	Sgt. JACK FERRIER		S/Sgt. JIMMY JACKSON
	Cpl. FRED GUERRA		
	Cpl. MANN THALER		

Production : T/Sgt. GEORGE VOUTSAS & Sgt. HARRY HARTWICK
Stage Manager : Sgt. JULIUS ZIFFERBLATT
Announcer : Cpl. PAUL DUBOV
Asst. Executive Officers : T/Sgt. JACK SANDERSON & Cpl. TOM COCHRAN

Above and below right: **Major Glenn Miller and the American Band of the Allied Expeditionary Force play** *In the Mood* **and Johnny Desmond** *(below left)* **sings a romantic number during the 1944 Jazz Jamboree at the Stoll, Kingsway, held on the** evening of Sunday, October 15. The performance was reputedly attended by 4,500 paying members of the public although that figure would appear to be questionable as the theatre could only seat 1,857 persons.

Above: **The Uptown Hall Gang fraternising with their British friends at the Feldman Swing Club on Sunday, September 3, 1944. Back row (L-R): drummers Carlo Krahmer, Sergeant Ray McKinley and Maurice Burman. Front row: Trumpeter RAF Corporal Arthur Mouncey; guitarists Sergeant Carmen Mastren and Ivor Mairants; pianist Sergeant Mel Powell; saxist Billy Amstell; singer Beryl Davis; bassist Tommy Bromley; clarinet player Sergeant 'Peanuts' Hucko; singers Benny Lee and Johnny Green with the young drummer, Victor 'Kid Krupa' Feldman, aged ten.** *Below:* **Now the 100 Club, the traditions of the past are continued at No. 100 Oxford Street as London's premier live music centre.**

Feldman Swing Club

100 OXFORD STREET

The Feldman Swing Club in Oxford Street is one of the world's most famous jazz clubs, — even the address '100 Oxford Street' means one thing — Jazz with a capital 'J'.

Back in 1944, the club was owned by the Feldman family, the most famous being the 'Boy Wonder' drummer Victor Feldman, aged ten!

On the evening of Sunday, September 3, six members of Glenn Miller's American Band of the AEF jammed with the house band at the club, which included top British musicians, Carlo Krahmer, Billy Amstell, Victor Feldman and many others. The session was repeated again at the same venue on Sunday, September 17, when eight members of the orchestra joined the house band. The third occasion was on Sunday evening, October 15, when Mel Powell (piano) and 'Peanuts' Hucko (clarinet) played a session with Victor Feldman at the club but, more important for the paying customers, was the fact that Glenn was present in the audience.

Queensbury
All Services Club

OLD COMPTON STREET

The Prince Edward Theatre was opened in Old Compton Street, Soho, in 1930 but, due to the later unpopularity of its namesake, was renamed the Casino in 1936. *Above:* Here, servicemen queue to enter the Queensbury All Services Club in 1944. After its wartime interlude as a mecca of entertainment for service personnel, the theatre reverted to the Casino, becoming the Casino Cinerama in 1974. However, with a new Prince Edward, in 1978 it once again adopted its pre-war name and in 1992 it was completely refurbished *(below)*.

The Queensbury All Services Club in Old Compton Street, Soho, was perhaps the top performing and broadcasting venue for the services during the war years. The theatre had been loaned to the forces by the owners of the day, headed by the Marquis of Queensbury, Sir Simon Marks, and during 1944 it provided weekly shows by the top Allied entertainment of the period, such as The British Band of the AEF, The Canada Show (the Canadian Band of the AEF), Vera Lynn, Anne Shelton and Bing Crosby.

PROGRAMME

"VARIETY BAND BOX"

The American Band of the Supreme Allied Command

MAJOR conducted by
~~CAPTAIN~~ GLENN MILLER

Executive Officer Lt. Don W. Haynes

Piano	S/Sgt. Mel Powell	Crew Chiefs	Sgt. Steve Steck	Violins—continued
	Cpl. Jack Rusin		Cpl. Eugene Steck	Cpl. Milton Edelson
Drums	T/Sgt. Ray McKinley		Cpl. Arthur Malvin	Sgt. Dave Herman
	Cpl. Frank Ippolito		Cpl. Murray Kane	Cpl. Phil Cogliano
Guitar	Sgt. Carmen Mastren		Cpl. Lynn Allison	Cpl. Joseph Kowalewski
Bass	S/Sgt. Trigger Alpert	Saxophones	S/Sgt. Hank Freeman	Sgt. Dave Schwartz
	Cpl. Joe Shulman		Sgt. Michael Hucko	Cpl. Henry Brynan
Trumpets	M/Sgt. Zeke Zarchy		Sgt. Vince Carbone	Cpl. Earl Cornwell
	Sgt. Bob Nicols		Sgt. Jack Ferrier	P.F.C. Fred Ostrovsky
	Sgt. Whitey Thomas		Cpl. Fred Guerra	Cpl. Morris Bialkin
	Sgt. Bernie Priven		Cpl. Mann Thaler	Cpl. Bob Ripley
	Cpl. Jack Steele			Cpl. Stanley Harris
Trombones	Sgt. Jimmy Priddy	French Horns	Cpl. Addison Collins, Jnr.	Cpl. Emanuel Wishnow
	Cpl. John Halliburton	Violins	S/Sgt. George Ockner	Cpl. Dave Sackson
	Cpl. Larry Hall		S/Sgt. Harry Katzman	Cpl. Nate Kaproff
	P.F.C. Nat Peck		Cpl. Ernest Kardos	Cpl. Richard Motolinski
			Cpl. Eugene Bergen	Arrangers T/Sgt. Jerry Gray
Vocalist	Sgt. Johnnie Desmond		S/Sgt. Carl Swanson	M/Sgt. Norm Layden
				S/Sgt. Ralph Wilkinson
				Sgt. Jimmy Jackson

Production S/Sgt. George Vontsas and Sgt. Harry Hartwick   Stage Manager Cpl. Julius Zifferblatt
Programme Director T/Sgt. Paul Dudley   Announcer Cpl. Paul Dubov
Assistant Executive Officers T/Sgt. Jack Sanderson and Cpl. Tom Cochran
By permission of Colonel E. M. Kirby, Director of SHAEF Broadcasting Service.

TEDDY BROWN
The Music Hall Xylophone Star

BERTHA WILMOTT
The North Country Chorus Singer

PETER SINCLAIR
Cock o' the North

HAL MONTY
Resident Comedian of "Variety Band Box"

JOHN BLORE AND HIS DANCE ORCHESTRA

M.C.: MARGARET LOCKWOOD—Star of "The Lady Vanishes," "The Man in Gray" and other Films
Editor: CECIL MADDEN   Producer: STEPHEN WILLIAMS

DANCING to HAL KENT'S BAND

Producer for the Queensberry All-Services Club: John Harding

The first performance by Glenn and the band at the All Services Club was on Sunday, July 30 when they appeared on the BBC radio show, *Variety Bandbox*. Based on requests from service personnel, the weekly programme went out over the air before an audience comprising entirely of servicemen and women. The programme sheet *(above)* gives details of the other acts that appeared with the band at the Queensbury that day.

The group photograph *(below)* was taken at rehearsals — from L-R: Stephen Williams, the programme's producer; Hal Monty, resident comedian; Cecil Madden, the editor; Bertha Willmott, singer; John Blore, the bandleader; Glenn Miller; Margaret Lockwood, who was the show's MC, and Peter Sinclair, the 'Cock o' the North', who was the guest comedian that week.

Above left: **Bing Crosby sings with Anne Shelton after the recording of** *Variety Bandbox* **at the Queensbury All Services Club on Sunday, August 27.** *Above right:* **The outstanding performance that autumn at the Queensbury has to be the combined AEF and US Navy Dance Band show on Thursday, September 21.**

Glenn Miller and his band first broadcast from this venue on the evening of Sunday, July 30, during the recording of the BBC's popular programme, *Variety Bandbox.*

The following month, on Sunday afternoon, August 27, as Glenn and the American Band of the AEF were playing at Twinwood Farm (see page 129), relief pianist Pfc Jack Russin with Glenn's producer, Paul Dudley, were travelling to London by staff car. Jack then recorded with Bing Crosby for *Variety Bandbox* at the Queensbury All Services Club, after which he played again with Bing and Anne Shelton in a special stage show at the club. Anne and Bing sang *Easter Parade* and joked around and the audience loved every minute of it!

The following Saturday, September 2, Glenn and the band gave a special forces' concert at the Queensbury. This was to become a regular event before and after their BBC-AEF broadcasts started later in the month. The first regular broadcasts by the Glenn Miller orchestra began here on the evening of Thursday, September 14, and continued right through October and November until December 12. The broadcasts from September 14 to October 26, featured a variety of British guest stars such as Paula Green (September 14); Pat Kirkwood (September 28); George Melachrino (October 5); Jack Hylton (October 12); Sally Douglas (October 19); and Anne Shelton (October 26). The September 21 broadcast and stage show was perhaps the most outstanding because it featured Sam Donahue and the US Navy Dance Band of the Liberation Forces. It was a night to be remembered and would hold a special place in many memories for years afterwards.

Pat Kirkwood recalls her guest spot on September 28 with affection. 'I was very nervous, having worshipped the great Glenn Miller for years. I found him a most quiet, charming and courteous man although, at rehearsal, he quietly suggested an alteration in the score which nearly, but not quite, threw me as I had sung the song as it was for

Centre: **Major Glenn Miller talking to British bandleader Harry Roy in the Dress Circle Bar on Thursday, September 28, 1944. British bandleader Jack Hylton (extreme left) looks on.** *Right:* **Today, the bar is little altered as Geoff Woodcock and Dominika Madej enjoy a drink on the same spot.**

PROGRAMME

Monday, December 11th
"YOU'VE HAD IT," REVUE GIVEN BY 540 COAST REGIMENT by permission of LT./COL. J. H. W. RICHARDS, O.B.E., R.A., with MAJORS MALLINSON and BOARDMAN, GNRS. WATSON, MORRIS, McCLEAN, CPL. DAVIES and L/BDR. BIRD
Produced by GNR. WATSON
DANCING TO HAL KENT'S BAND

Tuesday, December 12th

THE AMERICAN BAND OF THE A.E.F.
conducted by
MAJOR GLENN MILLER
Executive Officer Lt. Don W. Haynes
Programme Director W.O. Paul Dudley.

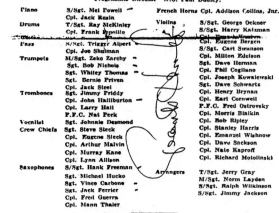

Piano	S/Sgt. Mel Powell
	Cpl. Jack Rusin
Drums	T/Sgt. Ray McKinley
	Cpl. Frank Ippolito
Bass	M/Sgt. Trigger Alpert
	Cpl. Joe Shulman
Trumpets	M/Sgt. Zeke Zarchy
	Sgt. Bob Nichols
	Sgt. Whitey Thomas
	Sgt. Bernie Priven
	Cpl. Jack Steel
Trombones	Sgt. Jimmy Priddy
	Cpl. John Halliburton
	Cpl. Larry Hall
	P.F.C. Nat Peck
Vocalist	Sgt. Johnnie Desmond
Crew Chiefs	Sgt. Steve Steck
	Cpl. Eugene Steck
	Cpl. Arthur Malvin
	Cpl. Murray Kane
	Cpl. Lynn Allison
Saxophones	S/Sgt. Hank Freeman
	Sgt. Michael Hucko
	Sgt. Vince Carbone
	Sgt. Jack Ferrier
	Cpl. Fred Guerra
	Cpl. Mann Thaler

French Horns Cpl. Addison Collins, Jnr.
Violins S/Sgt. George Ockner
S/Sgt. Harry Katzman
Cpl. Eugene Bergen
S/Sgt. Carl Swanson
Cpl. Milton Edelson
Sgt. Dave Herman
Cpl. Phil Cogliano
Cpl. Joseph Kowalewski
Sgt. Dave Schwartz
Cpl. Henry Brynan
Cpl. Earl Cornwell
P.F.C. Fred Ostrovsky
Cpl. Morris Binikin
Cpl. Bob Ripley
Cpl. Stanley Harris
Cpl. Emanuel Wishnow
Cpl. Dave Sackson
Cpl. Nate Kaproff
Cpl. Richard Motolinski

Arrangers
T/Sgt. Jerry Gray
M/Sgt. Norm Layden
S/Sgt. Ralph Wilkinson
S/Sgt. Jimmy Jackson

Production T/Sgt. George Voutsas and Sgt. Harry Hartwick
Stage Manager Sgt. Julius Zifferblatt
Announcer Cpl. Paul Dubov
Assistant Executive Officers T/Sgt. Jack Sanderson and Cpl. Tom Cochran

DANCING TO HAL KENT'S BAND

Thursday, December 14th
DANCING TO TOMMY KEMP'S BAND

Friday, December 15th
CARNIVAL NIGHT — SAM DONAHUE'S U.S. NAVY BAND
DANCING TO TOMMY KEMP'S BAND

Saturday, December 16th
GERALDO AND HIS ORCHESTRA with LEN CAMBER, SALLY DOUGLAS, PAT FROST and CELIA LIPTON
DANCING TO NED WHITEBREAD'S BAND

Sunday, December 17th
R.A.F. SKYROCKET'S ORCHESTRA with URIEL PORTER, MORTON FRAZER, TALBOT O'FARRELL, ELSIE CARLISLE, PATRICIA MORNE, A.T.S. GIRL PIPERS

M.C. : PATRICIA MEDINA
(The British Film Star)

Important Notice to Members
It has been brought to the Club Management's notice that some members are still allowing their Cards to be used by non members.
It is hoped that members will co-operate with us by showing their Identity Cards when asked in order that we may stamp out this unfair method of depriving a member of a seat by the misuse of a Membership Card.

Producer for the Queensberry All-Services Club : JOHN HARDING

The last Queensbury All Services Club programme for Major Glenn Miller's American Band of the Allied Expeditionary Force.

some time. I remember being a bit put out as the actual performance was close. He must have noticed this because he laughed! But I sang the song *My Kind of Music* for the rehearsal and, to my utter surprise, when I finished the whole orchestra cheered and threw their instruments into the air — except the bass player of course! I was most touched by this display of approval and was less nervous on the show and succeeded in skipping through the new alteration with ease, earning an approving grin from Glenn himself!'

On November 13, the broadcasting schedule for Glenn Miller's American Band of the AEF was altered and their live broadcast on Thursday evenings was changed to two evenings per week: 30 minutes on a Tuesday and a further half-hour on Friday. Usually, both broadcasts went out live at 8.30 p.m. from the Queensbury Club before a packed audience of up 2,500 service personnel. However, Glenn missed the first two that week, due to the fact he was at SHAEF headquarters in Paris.

Another special performance held on Tuesday, December 12 included a special guest, Irish-American singing star Morton Downey. This was to be the farewell for the American Band of the AEF before it moved to Paris but it was also destined to be Glenn's final live broadcast. Coupled with his sad death, it inevitably gives this performance at the club a certain poignancy.

This is believed to be the last photograph ever taken of Glenn Miller as he checks scripts with Morton Downey at the Queensbury All Services Club on the evening of Tuesday, December 12, 1944.

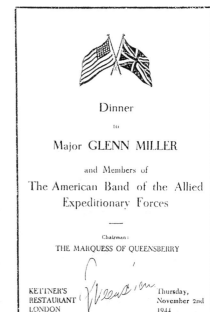

Bing Crosby with (L–R) British bandleader Geraldo, Sergeant Broderick Crawford, Pat Kirkwood, Colonel Ed Kirby, and BBC producer Cecil Madden, after a meal at Kettner's Restaurant in Romilly Street, on the evening of Sunday, August 27, 1944.

Menu from Kettner's Restaurant for the dinner on Thursday, November 2 — this copy from Glenn Miller's own files.

Kettner's Restaurant

ROMILLY STREET

Kettner's Restaurant in Romilly Street, just around the corner from the Queensbury All Services Club in Old Compton Street, has quite a history. Established in 1867, one of the best known stories about this famous West End restaurant occurred during the Second World War on the evening of Wednesday, August 30, 1944, during the height of the V1 flying bomb attack on London. Bing Crosby, on his first British tour, had been broadcasting at the Queensbury All Services Club with the British Band

of the AEF, under the direction of RSM George Melachrino. A large number of fans followed Crosby, who had met up with Glenn Miller, Don Haynes and Paul Dudley, to the restaurant. As the four Americans sat down for dinner, a large crowd gathered in the street outside for a glimpse of Bing Crosby, in spite of the fact that there was a law forbidding people to assemble together during the Blitz. They started to shout for their idol to appear whereupon Bing came to a first floor window and called to them: 'If I sing will you disperse?' The crowd agreed so he responded with two choruses of *Pennies from Heaven*. His impromptu audience gave him a tremendous ovation and then broke up in an orderly fashion.

On November 2, Miller and the entire band were the guests of honour at a special dinner in Kettner's hosted by Lord Queensbury (Sir Simon Marks). Among the guests present were Jack and Muriel Harding (the manager of the Queensbury All Services Club and his wife), Irish-American singer Morton Downey, British comedian Tommy Trinder, bandleader Jack Hylton and a niece of British Prime Minister, Winston Churchill.

One further occasion of note at the restaurant was a special farewell party arranged by Lord Queensbury following the band's final live broadcast and stage show at the Queensbury. Once again, among the special invited guests sitting down to dinner at 9.30 p.m., were Morton Downey and Tommy Trinder.

The night scene at Kettners (now usually spelt without the apostrophe) at No. 29 Romilly Street. The Prince Edward Theatre — the old Queensbury All Services Club — lies just a few dozen yards away in Old Compton Street.

Above: **Captain Miller directs the American Band of the Supreme Allied Command outside the manor house at Melchbourne** **Park on July 21, 1944, whilst** *(below)* **Sergeant Ray McKinley sings. The relief drummer, Frank Ippolito, stands behind.**

Melchbourne Park
Station 572

BEDFORDSHIRE

Melchbourne Park near Wellingborough, on the northern borders of Bedfordshire and Northamptonshire, was an Eighth Air Force ordnance depot. On Friday afternoon, July 21, 1944, Glenn Miller and the American Band of the Supreme Allied Command played a concert here for 750 officers and enlisted men. Don Haynes noted in his diary that 'the orchestra played outdoors on a platform alongside a hangar' and that 'it was in the mid-40's, and very cool'. As Haynes was not actually present at this concert, the diary entry was only partly correct. Miller and the orchestra did play outdoors on a platform, but in front of the headquarters which was located in the manor house in Melchbourne Park.

With the exception of Sergeant Mel Powell's Swing Sextet, which also included The Crew Chiefs singing group, who were scheduled to broadcast live at 6.15 p.m. that evening from Co-Partners Hall in Bedford, Glenn and the remainder of the orchestra stayed on after the concert for dinner and did not return to their quarters until 10 p.m.

Today, Melchbourne Park is a private estate comprising exclusive houses (including the old manor house) with restricted access.

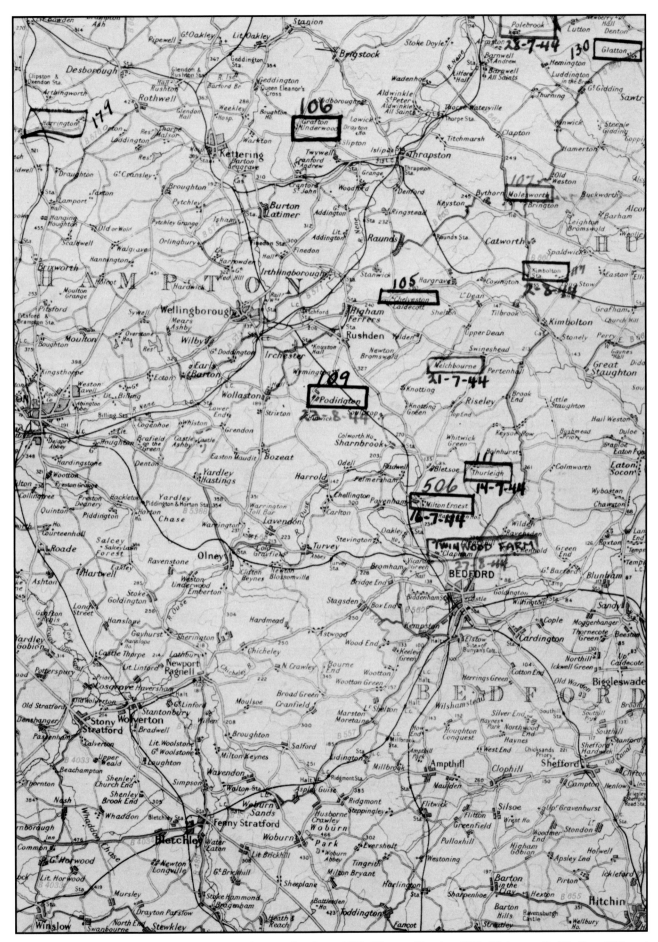

For some reason, Glenn has not added the station number for Melchbourne Park. The other five Eighth Air Force airfields shown: Harrington (Station 179), Grafton Underwood (Station 106), Glatton (Station 130), Molesworth (Station 107) and Chelveston (Station 105), all missed out on having concerts performed at their bases.

Milton Ernest Hall
Station 506

BEDFORDSHIRE

Milton Ernest Hall, five miles north of Bedford on the main A6 in the village of the same name, was taken over by the VIII Air Force Service Command during the late spring of 1943. Like the aerodrome at nearby Twinwood Farm, it features heavily in the last part of Glenn Miller's life and, of course, in the career of his famous band, initially called the American Band of the Supreme Allied Command but later renamed the American Band of the AEF.

When Miller and his band were moved out of London to the safety of Bedford, a problem arose: where could this large 60-man organisation have their meals? The American Red Cross Clubs in Bedford were too small and had inadequate mess areas, so Glenn and Don Haynes arranged with Brigadier General Donald R. Goodrich, the commander, for the orchestra to have their meals in one of the Nissen huts at Milton Ernest Hall that was used as a mess. In return for this hospitality, Miller arranged for Sergeant Ray McKinley and a quartet to perform at a special officers' club dance on the evening of Saturday, July 8, and for the entire band to play in the grounds at 4 p.m. on the afternoon of Sunday, July 16. The concert was an outstanding success, with 1,600 officers, enlisted personnel and civilian guests from the village present.

This was the start of a long association between General Goodrich and his staff with Glenn Miller and the members of the orchestra throughout their stay in England. One officer from Milton Ernest Hall who struck up a particularly close friendship with both Miller and Haynes was Lieutenant Colonel Norman F. Baessell, General Goodrich's Executive Officer. However, this association with Baessell and the latter's love of 'contacts' and 'fixing' would eventually lead to Glenn's demise, along with that of Baessell himself, for it was he who arranged for the cross-Channel flight on December 15.

Milton Ernest Hall and its picturesque grounds with the River Ouse running

The close relationship of Milton Ernest Hall to several of the other important sites in our 1944 Glenn Miller 'tour' is shown on the map *right*. Bedford is less than five miles away with Twinwood Farm aerodrome lying in between. Thurleigh airfield, roughly the same distance to the north-east, was the scene of a full orchestra concert on July 14 and another show put on by the Swing Sextet on September 8.

Left: **Milton Ernest Hall, situated between the A6 trunk road and the River Ouse north of Bedford, pictured in 1944 when it was the headquarters of VIII Air Force Service Command, and** *(right)* **as a peaceful old people's home in 1995.**

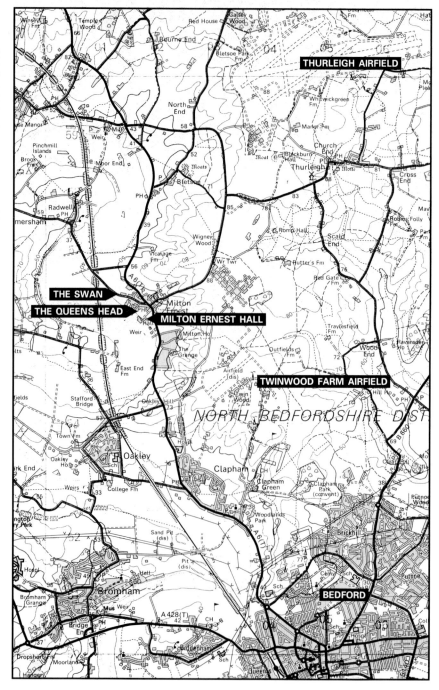

Above: Captain Glenn Miller conducts the American Band of the Supreme Allied Command in the grounds of Milton Ernest Hall on the afternoon of Sunday, July 16. *Below left:* Dorothy Carless sang for the headquarters' staff during the performance. *Below:* Today, the tranquil lawns belie the nostalgic aura of their upbeat past.

Just over a month later, it was the turn of Bing Crosby to be pictured at the hall. He is seen here on the terrace with a group of American officers on the evening of Tuesday, August 29, when he stayed overnight at Milton Ernest.

Don Haynes, Glenn Miller and an unidentified officer are served dinner by Sergeant Ming of the headquarters' catering staff.

From the downward-sloping view visible through the hut windows, we pinpointed the spot, still complete with the hut base, overlooking the river valley.

through it, provided overnight sleeping accommodation for two other visiting American singers; Dinah Shore, who stayed two nights in early August, and Bing Crosby on the night of Tuesday, August 29.

Six days after the July 16 concert, a small dance group from the Miller band performed at an officers' dance in the Officers' Mess at Milton Ernest Hall. Further groups played on and off at dances at the hall over the next five months. The string section from the American Band of the AEF even performed at a chapel service one Sunday morning (August 6). A special dance was held on the evening of Thursday, November 23, when Sergeant Ray McKinley and his famous Swing Shift (the orchestra's dance band unit) played at the Thanksgiving Day officers' dance at the hall.

It was at Milton Ernest Hall, while Don Haynes was having a meal with Lieutenant Colonel Baessell on Thursday, December 14, that Glenn rang through from the Mount Royal Hotel in London. During the conversation, Miller informed Haynes that all flights from Bovingdon had been cancelled due to the incredibly poor weather conditions and, consequently, he would not be able to precede the orchestra to France the following day. Baessell, overhearing the conversation, asked to speak to Miller and informed him that he was flying to Paris the next day and that Glenn was welcome to

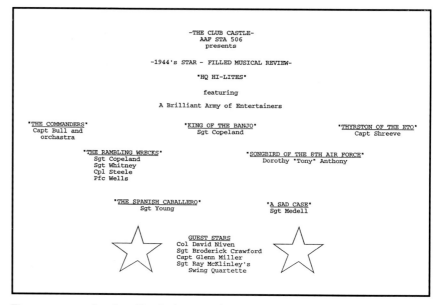

The programme for the officer's dance on Saturday evening, July 8.

travel with him. Glenn promptly instructed Haynes to get a staff car and pick him up that afternoon and take him back to Bedford.

Later that evening, Miller, Haynes, Baessell and two other officers played poker until the early hours of December 15 (see page 136).

After the war, Milton Ernest Hall first became an hotel before its current use as a retirement home. In latter years, a garden centre was established in the grounds. However, there is still much evidence remaining of the time it was the VIII Air Service Command HQ, including concrete pathways and hut bases. Even the ivy-clad boiler plant remains.

'We passed a building with a funny sign out front. It sounded like a party going on inside. I asked a passer-by what the celebration was about and promptly got introduced to a pub.'

So wrote one American serviceman on his discovery of a British institution which had no exact equivalent in his home country. Undoubtedly, the band would have concurred.

The Pubs

MILTON ERNEST

The village of Milton Ernest, on the main road north of Bedford, contains something of interest other than the now famous hall which was the VIII Air Force Service Command headquarters. The Swan, just off the A6 on the small country road to Radwell, was where members of the band used to drink after meals at Milton Ernest Hall. As they were very friendly with the Swan's landlord, Tom Larkin, they sometimes brought him bottles of scotch — a rare treat in rationed, wartime Britain.

The nearby Queens Head Hotel was also used by personnel from the adjacent HQ. It too, keeps the memories alive with framed pictures on the walls and, at Connie Richards suggestion, the dining room was named after Miller.

Then and now: Several pubs in the Bedford area claim an association with Glenn Miller, but the Queens Head Hotel *(top)* on the A6 in Milton Ernest and the nearby Swan *(above)* are the only ones where a connection can be confirmed.

Mount Farm Station 234

OXFORDSHIRE

Above: **Major Glenn Miller and the American Band of the AEF perform for the 7th PRG at Mount Farm on Monday, September 25, 1944.** *Below:* **Glenn failed to add the Mount Farm concert in his atlas so we have indicated the position of the airfield some 15 miles west of High Wycombe (page 54).**

Mount Farm airfield, eight miles south-east of Oxford, was opened in 1940 as a satellite base for the photographic reconnaissance unit at RAF Benson and was taken over by a squadron of F-4 Lightning photographic aircraft of the USAAF in February 1943. On March 7 that year, the Eighth Air Force formed its 7th Photographic Reconnaissance Group, consisting of the 13th, 14th, 22nd and 27th Photographic Squadrons, basing them at Mount Farm, thus continuing the airborne reconnaissance tradition at the airfield.

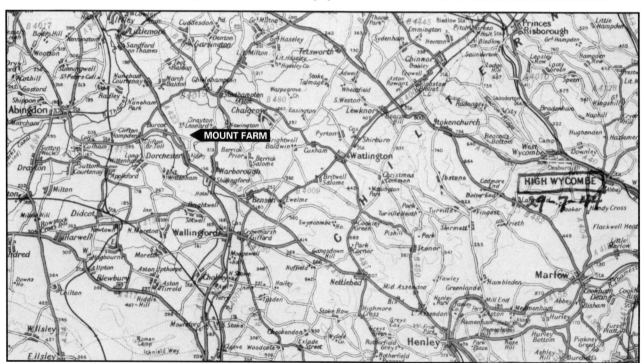

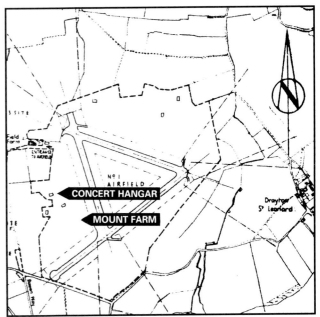

Above left: **The Crew Chiefs singing group also appeared (from L-R): Pfc Lynn Allison; Pfc Gene Steck; Corporal Murray Kane; Corporal Artie Malvin and Sergeant Steve Steck.**

On the evening of Monday, September 25, Glenn Miller and his band played in the same hangar where Bob Hope had performed over a year earlier with Francis Langford, some 3,500 officers and enlisted personnel being present. Due to the autumn weather, and with the nights drawing in, Miller and the orchestra had used road transport to travel to the base. They returned the same way, but due to the wartime black-out, the drivers got lost and they did not arrive back at their billets in Bedford until 2 a.m. the next morning.

During his brief stay at Mount Farm, Glenn was entertained by Brigadier General Elliott Roosevelt, the President's son, at Mount Farm *(right)*, situated on the south-western side of the airfield. Roosevelt had been put in charge of the 325th Photographic Reconnaissance Wing (encompassing the 7th PRG at Mount Farm and the 25th PRG at Watton) the previous month.

The 7th PRG pulled out of Mount Farm on May 1, 1945, when the airfield reverted to the RAF. It was later used by the Ministry of Supply for ex-WD vehicle sales, the site being sold in 1957. Today, apart from the perimeter track, the land has reverted to agriculture, the technical site having been swallowed up with the expansion of Berinsfield village. Nigel Dawe established that the blister hangar where the band played stood here, right in the middle of the new estate.

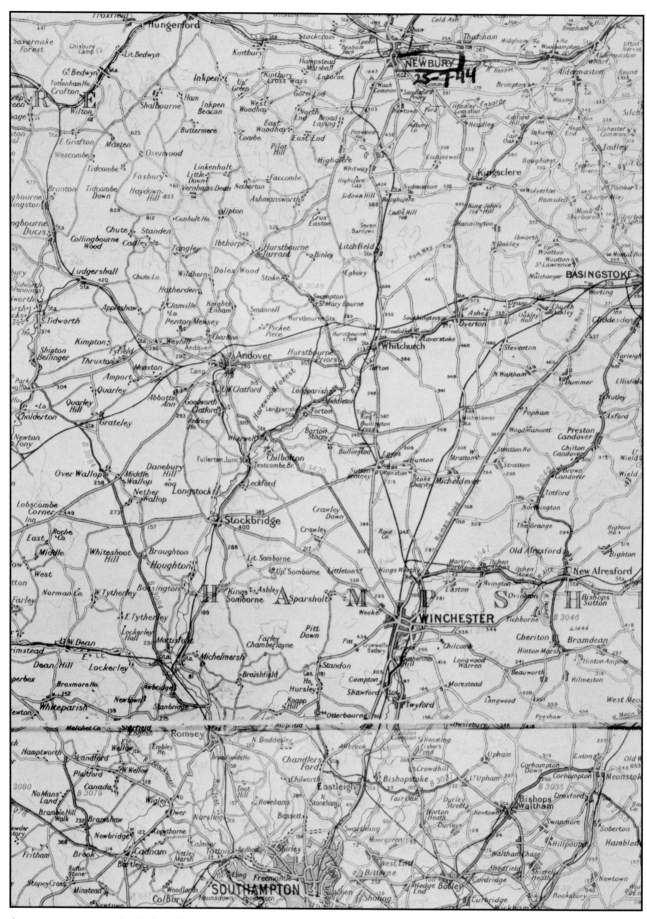

Just over two months before D-Day, the 101st Airborne Division lost its beloved commander, Major General William C. 'Bill' Lee, who had brought the division to Europe in 1943. He suffered a heart attack on February 5, 1944 and, instead of the Assistant Division Commander being promoted to take over, Major General Maxwell D. Taylor was brought in from the rival 82nd Airborne Division. Thus, when the division was relieved, having suffered 3,800 casualties in Normandy, it was General Taylor who greeted Glenn and the band at the special concert given for the 101st at Newbury.

The Corn Exchange

NEWBURY, BERKSHIRE

At 7.30 p.m. on the evening of Tuesday, July 25, Glenn Miller and the American Band of the Supreme Allied Command played a concert at the Newbury Corn Exchange for the men of the 101st Airborne Division (the Screaming Eagles) based in the Newbury area. The division had just returned from Normandy, having taken part in the D-Day airborne landings during which it sustained heavy casualties.

The Corn Exchange was filled to capacity that evening and loudspeakers had to be set up for the music to be relayed to the overspill gathered in the Market Place. Captain Miller and the band were introduced to the audience by General Maxwell D. Taylor, the Commanding General of the 101st. Miller and the orchestra had already performed at Greenham Common airfield, two miles from Newbury, that afternoon for the personnel of the Ninth Air Force Transport Command based there (see page 47).

Invitation to Dance to

Capt. Glen Miller & His Band

Honoring Men of the

AIRBORNE EAGLE DIVISION

Corn Exchange   25th July, 1944

Newbury   1930 Hours

This Invitation will admit one lady friend without charge

Unfortunately, no pictures of the actual concert have been traced so this 1933 shot *(above)* **of the Annual Children's Music Festival and the rather poor 1946 exterior view** *(below)* **must suffice to illustrate the venue where it was held.**

Today, the Corn Exchange in Newbury is still very much in use for concerts and dances, this picture being taken in October 1995.

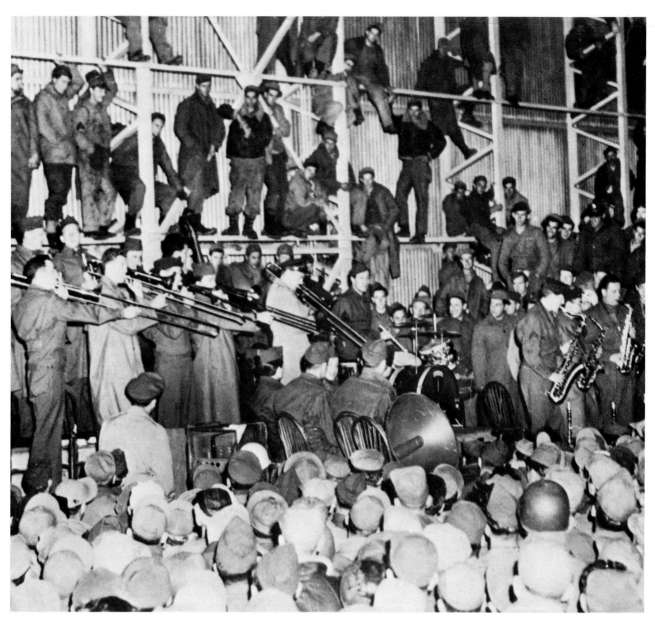

North Witham Station 479

LINCOLNSHIRE

North Witham airfield, 8½ miles south of Grantham, was opened in 1942 having been built as an RAF bomber base but was allocated to the USAAF Troop Carrier Command in August 1943. It was ultimately used as the 1st Tactical Air Depot belonging to the Air Force Service Command.

Between 1 and 2 p.m. on Sunday, September 24, 1944, Glenn Miller and the American Band of the AEF laid on a special concert here for airborne troops. It turned out to be a very cold day, and Miller and orchestra had to perform in overcoats, caps and gloves in the open-ended hangar. Afterwards, they travelled eight miles up the Great North Road to Grantham to give a second concert in the town's State Theatre (see page 44).

Above: **Major Glenn Miller and the American Band of the AEF, playing in No. 1 Hangar at North Witham airfield** *(right)*, **which lies just off the A1 near Grantham, on Sunday, September 24, 1944. Miller is the last trombonist from the left wearing the peaked cap and light overcoat. All the orchestra were well wrapped up for what proved to be one of their coldest performances.**

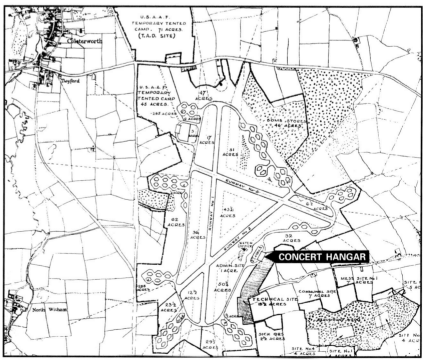

North Witham is unusual in that the whole of the old airfield is now covered with Forestry Commission woodland. However, the runways which form convenient firebreaks, the derelict control tower, and the old technical site off Honeypot Lane, are all owned by Witham (Specialist Vehicles) Ltd. The T2 hangar in which the concert was held still stands although the end has been reclad with smaller doors. However, the interior now presents a remarkable sight with row upon row of ex-British military vehicles awaiting new owners, our comparison being taken while perched on the turret of a Chieftain tank!

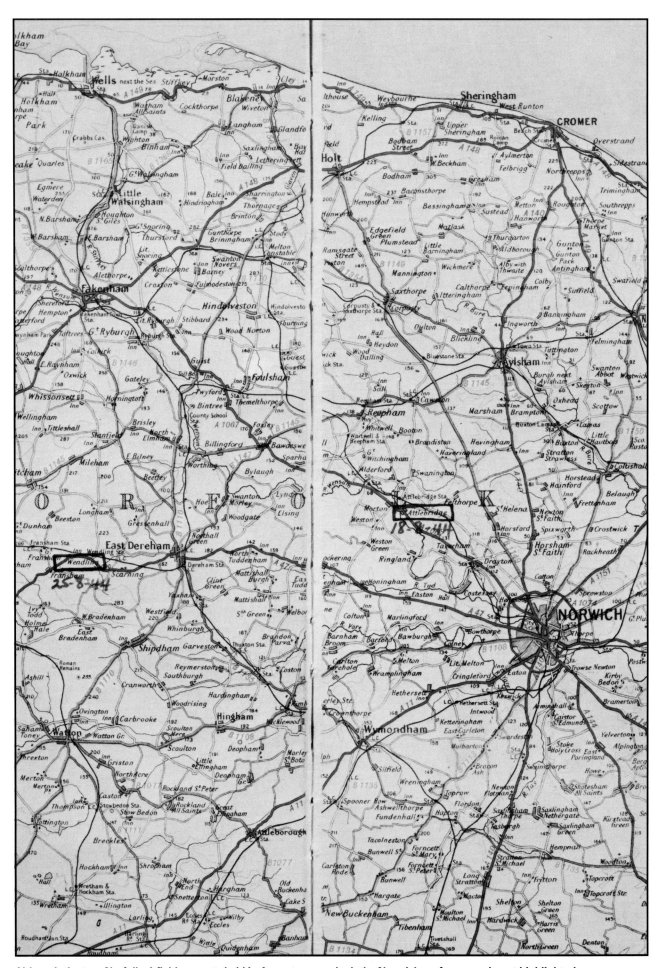

Although the two Norfolk airfield concerts held in August are marked, the Norwich performance is not highlighted.

Samson and Hercules Ballroom

NORWICH, NORFOLK

On the evening of Friday, August 18, having given the concert at Attlebridge air-field that afternoon (see page 18), Glenn and the dance band were taken by road into Norwich. There, at around 10.30 p.m. they played in the Samson and Hercules Ballroom on Tombland. Precise details about this concert and dance remain obscure, apart from the fact that Glenn and the musicians returned to Attlebridge that same night. They returned to Bedford on Saturday morning, August 19.

Norwich's Samson and Hercules Ballroom — so named after the statues which stood either side of the entrance — was the venue for the dance band on Friday, August 18. Here, Superintendent Charlie Baker directs the traffic outside on Tombland. Directly opposite stands Norwich Cathedral within whose grounds lies the grave of Nurse Edith Cavell, executed by the Germans in 1915.

In the 1940s, the dance hall was popularly known as the 'House of Muscles' but in the 1990s it's the Ritzy nightclub.

Long gone is the big band sound of Glenn Miller, replaced by the musical tastes of a younger generation.

Nuthampstead Station 131

HERTFORDSHIRE

Nuthampstead 5½ miles south-east of Royston, was built by the US Army and opened in 1943. The airfield was somewhat of an anachronism, in that it was one of the

Above: **Sergeant Ray McKinley conducts the American Band of the AEF during the concert held at Nuthampstead airfield for the 398th Bomb Group on the afternoon of October 2, 1944. (Earlier that morning, the group had been on an operation to Kassel.) Although reportedly attended by 3,000, the photo appears to indicate that figure to be an over-estimation, as may be the case with several other contemporary claims of audience numbers. Nuthampstead was taken over by the RAF in July 1945 and closed in 1959. The concert was held in the southernmost of the two T2 hangars on the technical site, now part of the Scales Park Estate owned by Robert Dimsdale.** *Below:* **Although the hangar itself has been dismantled, the base remains.**

Above: **After the concert, Don Haynes (extreme right) and Ray McKinley were pictured with two officers in the Officers' Club.** *Bottom:* **This was located in Site No. 3 which once occupied this ploughed field opposite White's Farm on the road from Nuthampstead to Barkway.**

nearest Eighth Air Force heavy bomber bases to London but also one of the most isolated, being situated in a sparsely populated area of northern Hertfordshire.

The first unit stationed here from September 1943 was the 55th Fighter Group, but this unit moved out to Wormingford in Essex during April 1944 to make way for the 398th Bomb Group.

On Monday, October 2, Glenn Miller was otherwise engaged so the American Band of the AEF was conducted in his absence by their drummer, Sergeant Ray McKinley. The concert for 3,000 officers and enlisted personnel was held between 3 and 4.30 p.m. in the main hangar and, afterwards, the orchestra were given dinner at the base.

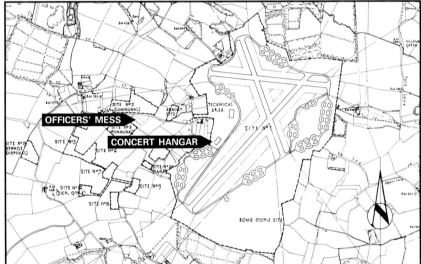

91st General Hospital

OXFORD

Major Glenn Miller and the American Band of the AEF perform *In the Mood* at the 91st General Hospital in Oxford on Monday afternoon, September 25, 1944. Now the Churchill Hospital, a plaque records its former use as the 2nd General Hospital from July 1942 to April 1944 and the 91st General Hospital from April 1944 to April 1945.

On Monday afternoon, September 25, 1944, after travelling by road from Bedford, Glenn and the band gave an open-air concert on the lawn at the 91st General Hospital situated just north of Southfield Golf Course in Oxford. It was a cold day and this performance, which began at 3.30 p.m., before an audience of 1,200 patients, nurses and doctors, lasted for an hour.

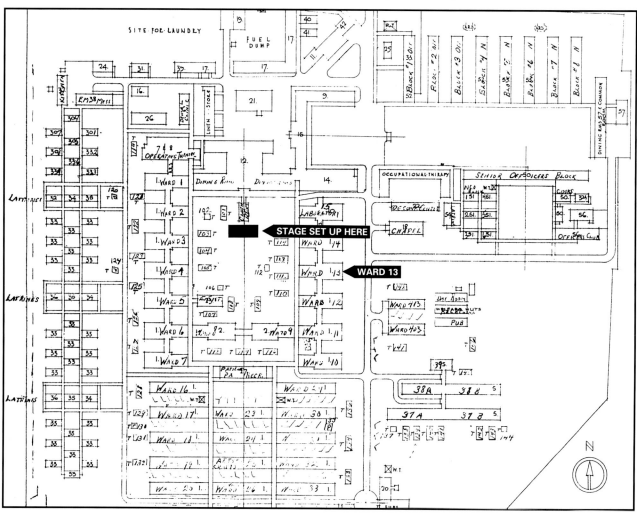

Above: **The grass quadrangle normally used for baseball by staff and inmates, was chosen as the site for the concert.** **Today, it is but a quarter of its original size as additional hospital facilities have encroached to fill it up.**

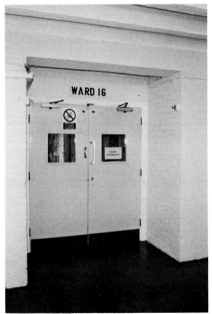

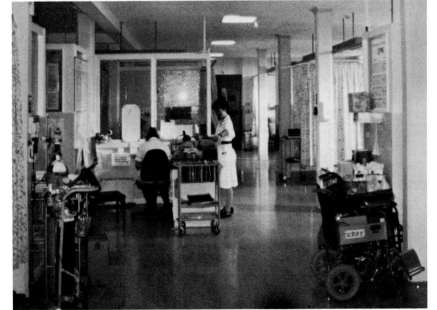

Above: **One consequence of post-war alterations is that Wards 12 and 13 have now been combined to form a new ward, No. 16.** *Above right:* **During the war, Ward 13 served the burns unit and Mary Clark, one of the nurses there, remembered her meeting with Glenn Miller in September 1944. After the concert was over, she went up to Major Miller and, explaining that all her patients were bedridden, asked him if he would come and play on the ward for them. Readily agreeing, Miller grabbed a selection of band members and played for about 20 minutes in Ward 13. Afterwards, noting that he seemed rather pale, Mary asked Glenn if he was feeling alright. He replied, in the affirmative, but asked how ever did she stand the unpleasant odour? Mary replied that she was trained for that whereupon Glenn responded by stating that he would not want her job for anything!**

Fifty years after the Churchill opened as a US military hospital, vehicles of the Ridgeway Military & Aviation Research Group returned for an historic photograph.

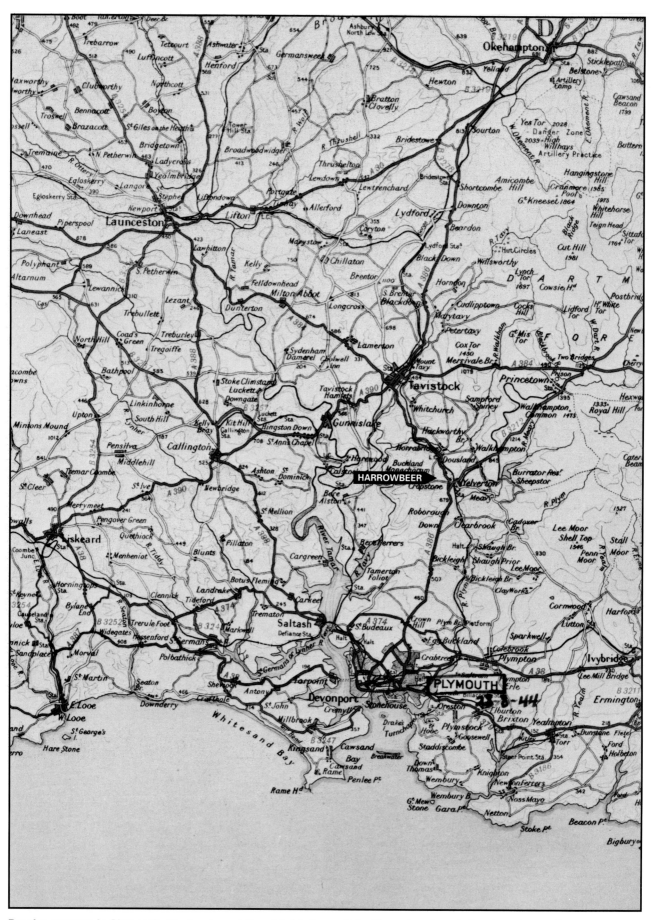

For the concerts in Plymouth, the band used the airfield at Harrowbeer (we have indicated its position north of the city). Over the previous months, it had seen much activity during the invasion but by late August when Glenn and the band arrived, it was too far from the battle-zone and all RAF operational units had been transferred elsewhere. It was then mainly being used by communications aircraft of the US Navy visiting the Fleet Air Wing HQ. At one period after the war, it was proposed to use it for Plymouth's airport but when Roborough was chosen instead, Harrowbeer was dismantled.

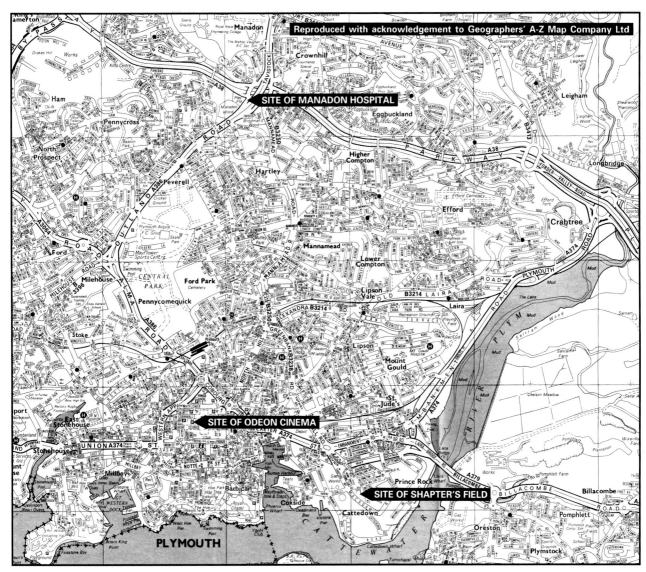

SITE OF MANADON HOSPITAL

SITE OF ODEON CINEMA

SITE OF SHAPTER'S FIELD

PLYMOUTH

Plymouth

DEVONSHIRE

At noon on Monday, August 28, 1944, Glenn Miller and the American Band of the AEF were flown by C-47 transports of the Ninth Air Force from Twinwood Farm to the RAF airfield at Harrowbeer on the edge of the Dartmoor village of Yelverton. This whole trip to the south-west of England was bedevilled by bad weather. Glenn and the band were delayed in leaving Twinwood (they should have been picked up at 10.30 a.m. but did not leave until 12 noon) and, once they arrived, the orchestra ended up being stranded in Plymouth for two days.

After playing at three separate venues on Monday, they were scheduled to leave Plymouth the next morning and fly to the fighter base at Wormingford in Essex. However, being grounded because of the foggy conditions, Miller and the band were forced to cancel and stay over in Plymouth until they could depart on Wednesday morning, August 30.

Major Glenn Miller pictured on his arrival at RAF Harrowbeer on Monday, August 28, 1944.

Out of all the Plymouth venues 'worked' by the band, Harrowbeer aerodrome *(above)* is probably the least altered, in spite of the fact that it has largely been demolished. The town locations have, without exception, completely disappeared.

US Navy Field Hospital

MANADON, PLYMOUTH

The US Navy Field Hospital at Manadon was opened on Saturday, February 12, 1944. As well as providing medical care for the thousands of US troops in the area during the build-up for the invasion, it was built to

The entrance to the US Navy Field Hospital at Manadon, Plymouth, October 11, 1944.

After the war, the huts were taken over by the Ministry of Works for a hostel but now an office block for the South West Electric Board occupies the site. Manadon Hill is still visible on the skyline *(below)*, matching that in the wartime view of the entrance *(above)*, although the ground level of the SWEB car park has been lowered.

Glenn at the hospital on the afternoon of Monday, August 28. The tree looks much like the right hand one in the picture, *above right*.

handle the expected intake of casualties from the Normandy landings. It was under the command of Commander K. R. Weston and had an X-Ray, dental, surgical, orthopaedic, traumatic and ear, nose and throat departments. Initially, the hospital was only equipped with 250 beds although it was planned to double this number if there was an influx of large numbers of casualties.

Above: **This aerial picture shows a large building at bottom right which may be the auditorium used for the concert.** *Below:* **Today, the Golden Hind pub and the two semi-detached houses in the middle distance still stand as useful reference points.**

On the afternoon of Monday, August 28, Glenn Miller and the dance band from the American Band of the AEF with Sergeant Ray McKinley on drums, singer Sergeant Johnny Desmond and The Crew Chiefs on vocals, gave a concert in the auditorium which was attended by 750 patients and staff. A second show for 600 was given early evening by the 20-piece string section directed by Staff Sergeant George Ockner.

Left: **Major Glenn Miller with Lieutenant Commander Robert A. Brown outside one of the Nissen huts at Shapter's Field in Plymouth on Monday afternoon.** *Right:* **The group shot, includes two US Navy officers at either end of the back row, with Miller,** **Don Haynes and Commander Brown in the middle. Three Ninth Air Force officers kneel in the foreground.** *Below:* **Queen Anne's Barracks, where the band were billeted during their Plymouth tour, still stands today converted into flats.**

Shapter's Field
(Queen Anne's Barracks)

PLYMOUTH

During the late afternoon of Monday, August 28, Glenn, together with Sergeant Ray McKinley and his dance band (better known as the Swing Shift) gave a concert for 750 US Navy and Seabee personnel at Shapter's Field, not far from Queen Anne's Barracks, where the band was billeted while in Plymouth. After the concert, Miller and Don Haynes had dinner with the base commander, Lieutenant Commander Robert A. Brown, USNR, who had taken over the base two months earlier.

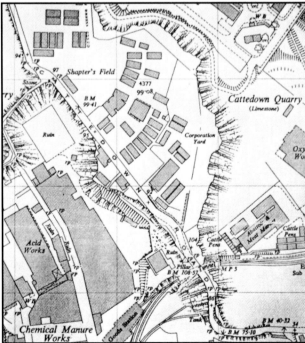

Shapter's Field lay just to the east of Cattedown Road but today the quarry has been extended westwards so that it now completely obliterates the site.

However, the new road which replaces Cattedown Road at this point has, with a sense of history, perpetuated the name.

Glenn signing autographs during the interval at the Odeon concert, August 28, 1944..

Odeon Cinema

PLYMOUTH

At 10.15 p.m. on Monday evening (August 28), Miller and the band gave a special concert for 4,000 Allied service personnel and civilians at the Odeon cinema which stood in the middle of a very badly bombed area of Plymouth. The local papers had announced that as well as Glenn and the orchestra being present, Bing Crosby would be with them; consequently, the cinema was packed to capacity. However, that evening Bing was performing with his small USO troop at the 78th Fighter Group base at Duxford airfield near Cambridge. In spite of this, people began queueing early and the scenes were reminiscent of a peacetime film premiere in London. So great was the crush that the beginning of the concert was delayed while the audience was ushered inside in small groups.

Glenn and the band performed the following routine that evening, opening of course with their 'signature tune', *Moonlight Serenade*. *Juke-box Saturday Night* — vocal, The Crew Chiefs; *Holiday for Strings*; *One O'Clock Jump*; *In the Mood*; *Poinciana* — vocal, Johnny Desmond and The Crew Chiefs; *It Must be Jelly*; *Cow Cow Boogie* — vocal, Ray McKinley (also conducting); *Down the Road a-piece* — vocal, Ray McKinley and 'Trigger' Alpert; *G.I. Jive* — vocal, Ray McKinley and The Crew Chiefs; and *Anvil Chorus*. The concert finished at 11.45 p.m. with *God Save the King*.

Left: **Seen here not long before its demolition, the Odeon was pulled down in the early 1960s during an extensive redevelopment of this part of the blitzed city centre. Even George Street has now been renamed New George Street.** *Above:* **The side of Littlewoods now follows the wall of the cinema auditorium. The front door of the Odeon would have been immediately to the left of this subway.**

Above: **Glenn Miller with Colonel William E. Reid, the 92nd's CO, and other officers** *(right)* **pictured at Podington on the afternoon of August 23, 1944 — a day when bad weather cancelled all bomber operations over the Continent.**

Podington Station 109

BEDFORDSHIRE

Podington airfield, some six miles south-east of Wellingborough, was originally built and opened for RAF use in 1942 and was among a batch of newly-completed airfields that were transferred to the Eighth Air Force in the spring of the same year. It was occupied by various bomber units until the oldest of the Eighth's bomb groups, the 92nd — 'Fame's Favored Few' — moved in from Alconbury in September 1943.

On Wednesday afternoon, August 23, 1944, from 2.30 to 4.00 p.m., Major Glenn Miller and the American Band of the AEF gave a 90-minute open-air concert for 2,500 officers and enlisted personnel of the 92nd. A makeshift stage comprising flat-bed trailers had been set up on a purpose-built hardstand in the No. 2 Communal site called the 'Arena', which was used for boxing tournaments and other concerts, as well as parades, etc. After the show at Podington, Miller and the band were then flown in B-17s to Framlingham airfield in Suffolk.

The concert was not held on the airfield but in Communal Site No. 2, normally the venue for more mundane events like boxing.

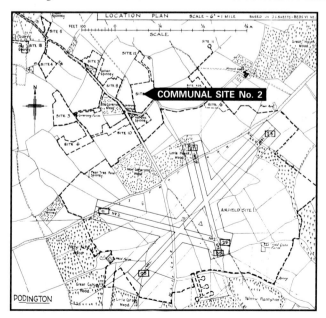

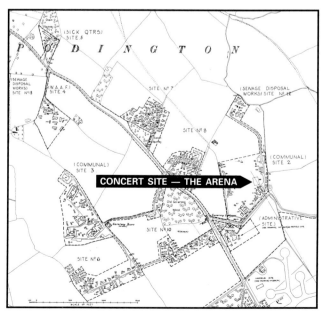

Above: **Glenn directs the orchestra as Sergeant Bobby Nichols solos on trumpet, and** *(right)* **introduces a number for the crowd.** *Below:* **Today, Podington is better known in the drag-racing world as Santa Pod which takes place on the old main runway. Many of the original buildings still remain, including the control tower, although both hangars have gone. 'The Arena' — laid as a self-help project by 92nd Bomb Group personnel — was located at the bottom of a gradual incline, ideal for unobstructed viewing and it was here that two flat-bed trailers were parked for the band. Unfortunately the concrete has since been removed, the site now lying within the entrance to the fishing bait works of Bedford (Brand) Supplies Ltd.**

Polebrook Station 110

NORTHAMPTONSHIRE

Polebrook was opened in 1941 for the RAF but was turned over to the Eighth Air Force in the summer of 1942. It was first occupied by the 97th Bomb Group — the first USAAF heavy bomber group to reach Britain — which carried out the first Eighth Air Force mission in Europe on August 17, 1942. In the summer of 1943, Captain Clark Gable, the Hollywood film star, was based at Polebrook for the making of a gunnery training film, *Combat America*, with the 351st Bomb Group which had arrived in April that year.

On Friday, July 28, 1944, Glenn Miller and the American Band of the Supreme Allied Command arrived at Polebrook to give a concert for 2,500 officers and enlisted personnel of the 351st. That morning, the group had visited Merseburg in eastern Germany but they returned in time for the late afternoon performance held in the J-type hangar.

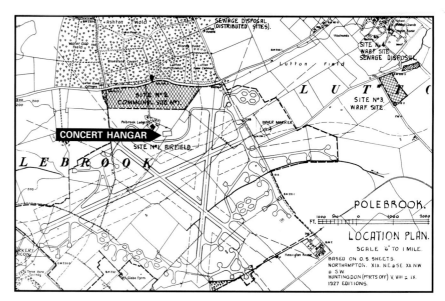

Sold by the Air Ministry in 1965, today much of Polebrook has disappeared, its runways sacrificed for hardcore, and the airfield returned to agriculture — apart, that is, from a solitary remaining hangar, fortuitously the very same one used for the band's performance on that late summer afternoon in 1944.

It was purchased by David Gower in 1981 and now lies within the perimeter of his company, Potato Consultants. David is an honorary member of the 351st Bomb Group Association, and has met many veterans returning to 'their' airfield, but still no trace of a photograph of the concert that day has come to light.

SHAEF Main HQ Station 586

On the afternoon of Wednesday, August 9, 1944, the Miller band gave a concert at 'Widewing' — by then the Rear HQ of SHAEF — in Bushy Park, Teddington.

BUSHY PARK, TEDDINGTON

On February 22, 1943, USAAF Station 586 in Bushy Park, Teddington, was officially dedicated and named after Lieutenant Colonel Townsend Griffiss who was the first American airman to lose his life on active service in Europe in the Second World War (see *After the Battle* No. 84). Camp Griffiss was initially the headquarters of the Eighth Air Force and the VIII Air Force Service Command, each situated in single-storey office blocks, bordering Sandy Lane on the north side of the park, which had originally been erected by the Ministry of Works as emergency accommodation for commercial firms bombed out of London.

In January 1944, with the appointment of General Dwight D. Eisenhower as Supreme Commander for Operation 'Overlord' to liberate Europe, a location was sought which would fulfil Eisenhower's requirement for an out-of-town headquarters for SHAEF. As the accommodation occupied by the Eighth Air Force at Bushy Park was available following its move to High Wycombe (see page 54), SHAEF Main Headquarters, code-named 'Widewing', was established in the park in March 1944, alongside the HQ buildings of Major General Carl Spaatz's US Strategic Air Force.

All the buildings in Bushy Park were demolished in the 1960s, but a tablet *(centre)* commemorating the tenure of Camp Griffiss by the USAAF was unveiled in 1945 by General Ira Eaker on the lawn where Glenn had played the previous year. In June 1994, as part of the Royal Parks' commemoration of the 50th anniversary of D-Day, a plaque was unveiled in Bushy Park to mark its use as the Supreme Headquarters of the Allied Expeditionary Force (see *After the Battle* No. 85). On this occasion, the 'big band' sound was provided by Opus One, although the stage was located on the site of the actual SHAEF buildings rather than the lawn in front of them where Miller played. *Right:* The 'forties dance group The GI Jitterbugs provided a touch of nostalgia.

SANDY LANE

SITE OF CONCERT

BLOCK C

EISENHOWER'S OFFICE

This 1947 aerial photograph shows the layout of the Bushy Park complex, pretty much unchanged in the immediate post-war period, save for the in-filling of air raid trenches. We have indicated the concert site on the left-hand lawn in front of Block C. Eisenhower had his office in the bottom right-hand corner of this block.

By the time Glenn Miller arrived in London at the end of June, many of the SHAEF staff were preparing to move to a Forward Headquarters at Portsmouth before crossing to France. Glenn spent several days at 'Widewing' before the arrival of his orchestra, planning locations for their billets, radio broadcasts and, above all, personal appearances at camps. When the band did get to London on June 29, Glenn and his Executive Officer, Don Haynes, drove out to Bushy Park to arrange the transfer to Bedford.

On the afternoon of Wednesday, August 9, Miller and the full 40-piece American Band of the AEF played for 3,000 SHAEF and air force staff on the lawn in front of the Officers' Club, 'Widewing' having now been redesignated SHAEF Rear HQ.

Part of the June 1994 commemoration in the park, which accompanied the unveiling of the SHAEF plaque, entailed the raising of a SHAEF flag on the site of Eisenhower's office — the flagpole can be seen centre right.

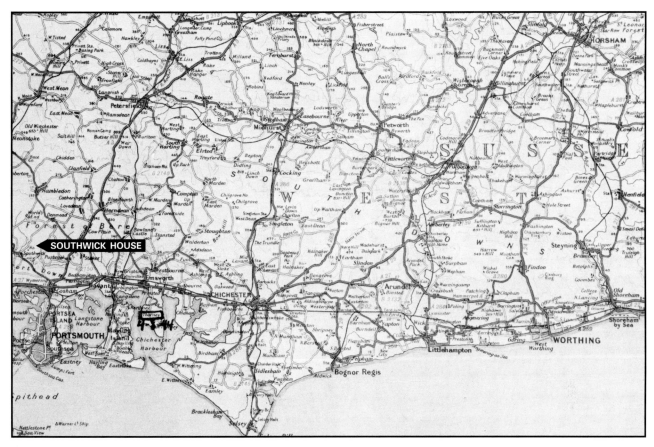

Southwick House, lying in its own secluded grounds, was the top secret headquarters on the south coast where the Allied commanders had carried out their final deliberations before D-Day. By August, SHAEF had moved its Forward HQ (code-named 'Shipmate') to the nearby Millard's Wood and General Eisenhower had a separate camp ('Sharpener') a mile from the house in Sawyer's Wood. Thus, the whole area was a top security zone and Glenn's atlas merely indicates the airfield to which they were flown — Thorney Island. (We have added an annotation to show the location of Southwick House.)

Southwick House

PORTSMOUTH, HAMPSHIRE

On Friday, August 4, 1944, Glenn Miller and the entire American Band of the AEF were collected from Twinwood Farm by three C-53 transport planes for an unknown destination. Several days beforehand, a staff officer from SHAEF Headquarters Command, Captain W. S. Sterns, had arranged with Don Haynes for Glenn and the band to play at an extra-special concert on August 4. For security reasons, Sterns said that he could not give Haynes the location and it was not until the planes had actually taken off that they were informed that they were to play at Southwick House, just outside Portsmouth. Nominally the headquarters of the Allied Naval Commander-in-Chief, Admiral Sir Bertram Ramsay, the mansion had been used by Eisenhower (whose own Advanced HQ was located in nearby woodland) before and during the D-Day landings (see *After the Battle* No. 84). Captain Sterns told Don Haynes that the General had personally asked for the band after he had heard several of their broadcasts.

The three aircraft landed at Thorney Island, the orchestra being taken in trucks and a staff car the ten miles to Southwick House, the whole area being guarded by military police.

The band set up in the open under camouflage netting with General Eisenhower and his staff sitting in the front row. They performed for about an hour to tremendous applause from an audience of around a thousand and, when the concert was over, the Supreme Commander congratulated Miller on the marvellous morale-boosting job he and the band were doing. Eisenhower also thanked Glenn for bringing the band down to play for him and his staff shortly before his Advanced HQ moved to France.

Glenn and the band were taken back to the airfield on Thorney Island and, as they were loading their equipment on to their aircraft, a C-47 landed nearby and out stepped a smartly-dressed German general, recently captured in Normandy. As Glenn and the band watched, he was quickly surrounded by six MPs and marched off to a waiting staff car and driven away!

The band were only told where they were to play that Friday after their aircraft had taken off and, due to the high security surrounding this special concert, no photographs are believed to have been taken. However, it is almost certain that it would have been held on the lawn at the rear of the house.

Whilst at RAF Thorney Island aerodrome, the band found time on their hands for a unique group photograph. From L-R (back row standing): Captain Glenn Miller, Hank Freeman, Al Milton (Edelson), Paul Dudley, Carl Swanson, Whitey Thomas, Jack Ferrier, Murray Kane, Vince Carbone, Dave Sackson, Johnny Halliburton, Bob Ripley, Bobby Nichols, Lynn Allison, Jack Steele, Julius Zifferblatt, Larry Hall, Dave Schwartz, Maurice Bialkin, Herman 'Trigger' Alpert, Phil Cogliano (Marino),

Addison Collins Jr, Jack Sanderson, Gene Bergen, Bernie Priven. Middle row: Henry Brynan, Mannie Thaler, Jimmy Priddy, Josef Kowalewski, Jimmy Jackson, Freddy Guerra, Dave Herman, George Ockner, Stan Harris, Carmen Mastren, Earl Cornwell. Front row: Johnny Desmond, Manny Wishnow, Freddy Ostrovsky, Ernest Kardos, Harry Katzman, Dick Motylinski, Frank Ippolito, Nat Peck, Artie Malvin, Zeke Zarchy, Michael 'Peanuts' Hucko, Nat Kaproff, Ray McKinley and Mel Powell.

Steeple Morden Station 122

CAMBRIDGESHIRE

Lying between the Cambridgeshire villages of Steeple Morden and Litlington, the airfield grew from a small satellite of Bassingbourn which lies just three miles to the north-east. The RAF handed it over to the USAAF and, from July 1943, the 355th Fighter Group operated out of Steeple Morden for two years, becoming the top-scoring US ground strafing unit by the war's end.

On the afternoon of August 18 — the day of the Attlebridge concert (see page 18) — four B-24s from the 466th Bomb Group at Attlebridge flew Major Glenn Miller and the American Band of the AEF down to Steeple Morden. The day before, Miller had been promoted, and a very rare colour cine film of Glenn at Steeple Morden was taken by Paul Chryst, a navigator with the 401st Bomb Squadron of the 91st Bomb Group at Bassingbourn, showing Glenn talking to officers shortly after his arrival at the fighter base.

The hour-long concert was staged in the hangar on the technical site, not only for the 355th Fighter Group but also for the 91st Bomb Group invited over from their nearby base. It was one of the largest performances by the band in Britain with an estimated

Above: **The afternoon of August 18, 1944 . . . and the newly-promoted Major Miller and his band fly into Steeple Morden in four B-24s of the 466th Bomb Group, including the group's assembly ship painted in bright zig-zag colours to assist being spotted by other aircraft in formation.**

Top left: **This clip from a colour cine film taken by Paul Chryst of the 401st Bomb Squadron of the 91st BG, shows Glenn with another officer beside the second B-24 from the right.** *Above:* **Today, the airfield, like so many others once occupied by the USAAF, is now just farmland, but if this land could talk what a story it would tell!**

The two Glenns at Steeple Morden. Lieutenant Colonel Glenn E. Williams, of the 355th Fighter Group with the station CO, Lieutenant Colonel Everett W. Stewart, and Glenn Miller at the eastern end of the single T2 hangar.

After the hangar was dismantled, Ken and Peter Jarman and their father uprooted part of the concrete at the eastern end; hence the comparison, with your Editor as stand-in, now has to be taken several yards out into his field of crops!

Major Glenn Miller and the American Band of the AEF perform *In the Mood* at Steeple Morden on Friday afternoon, August 18, 1944. Master Sergeant Zeke Zarchy performs the muted trumpet solo; Glenn is the third trombonist from the left. That morning, the 355th had been on escort duty to Paris when three of their aircraft had been shot down. However, Lieutenant Priest had landed his P-51 nearby and picked up one of the pilots, Lieutenant Marshall. Squashed in the cockpit, they arrived back at Steeple Morden just before the concert. As Don Haynes recorded in his diary, there was something else to celebrate that day! The hangar in which Glenn played was sold by the Air Ministry to a German buyer in the 1960s, the base now forming the foundation for various buildings at Ken and Peter Jarman's Goldmere Farm.

audience of some 5,000 officers and enlisted personnel. At 3.30 p.m., with the first notes of *Moonlight Serenade*, a huge roar went up as *In The Mood* was followed by other favourites, with Sergeant Johnny Desmond singing some of the romantic numbers.

The band stayed for dinner, after which the B-24s headed back to their home base in Norfolk for evening concerts by Glenn and the band at Attlebridge.

A small dance unit under Master Sergeant Zeke Zarchy returned to Steeple Morden on the evening of Saturday, August 26 to perform in the Officers' Club to an audience of around 500.

The Officers' Mess was located on dispersed Site B just to the west of Litlington village, now just a ploughed field belonging to Sharps Farm.

The small dance unit under Master Sergeant Zeke Zarchy at Steeple Morden on the evening of Saturday, August 26, 1944.

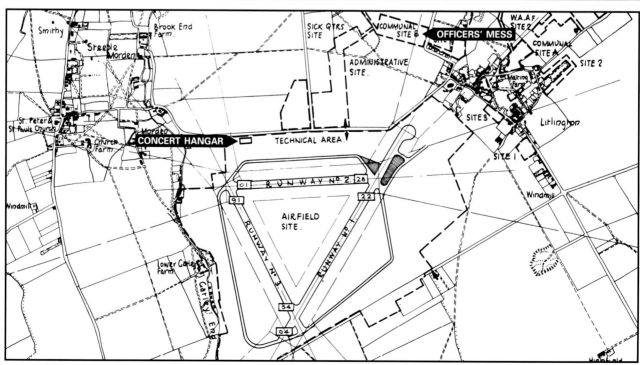

Glenn and the trombone section of the American Allied Expeditionary Force band perform their stage show *(above)* which usually accompanied their rendition of *In The Mood*. This almost obligatory number formed part of the programme to the concert at Thorpe Abbotts for the 'Bloody 100th' Bomb Group on the evening of Friday, September 1, 1944. After the show, Glenn met other officers for drinks in the Officers' Day Room, where he posed for this photograph *(below right)* with Colonel Thomas S. Jeffrey Jr and an unnamed nursing sister from the 65th General Hospital plus another unidentified officer. The 100th gained something of an undeserved reputation as a 'jinx' outfit within the Eighth Air Force, despite the fact that its losses were little different to other units. Doubtless the Miller concert provided welcome relief from their trials.

Thorpe Abbotts Station 139

NORFOLK

Thorpe Abbotts, built in 1942, was originally a satellite to Horham, but it was expanded into a main bomber base in its own right for the 100th Bomb Group.

The concert held here from 7 to 8 p.m. on Friday, September 1, 1944, was attended not only by the 100th, but also by their two sister bomb groups in the 13th Combat Wing: the 95th based at Horham and the 390th from Framlingham. Another unit invited from the Diss area was the 65th General Hospital. All told, some 3,000 were present in the main hangar at Thorpe Abbotts to hear Glenn and the American Band of the Allied Expeditionary Force perform *In The Mood* and all the other hits for the eager audience.

Earlier that day, the group had been recalled from an attack on Mainz due to bad weather; that evening the band also got weathered in at Thorpe Abbotts and decided to stay overnight before being taken to London on Saturday morning.

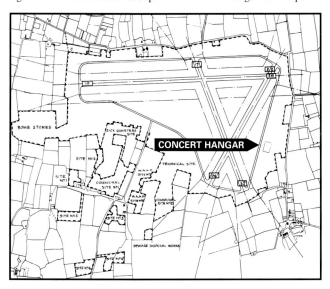

While Glenn Miller conducts, The Crew Chiefs sing *Juke-box Saturday Night*, while Bobby Nichols solos on trumpet, during the Thorpe Abbotts show. Some of the 65th General Hospital nurses who were invited can be seen sitting on the right.

Below: The easternmost T2 hangar in which the concert was performed was dismantled in the late 1950s; today the base is used for the dumping of hardcore and the storage of various road-making equipment.

Captain Glenn Miller with GIs outside the hangar at Thurleigh airfield just after the concert had finished on the afternoon of Friday, July 14, 1944.

Thurleigh Station 111

BEDFORDSHIRE

Thurleigh airfield, some six miles north of Bedford, was opened in 1941 and taken over by the USAAF's 306th Bombardment Group in September 1942.

On Thursday, July 6, 1944, Thurleigh was visited by members of the Royal Family, including HRH Princess Elizabeth. Eight days later, Captain Glenn Miller and the American Band of the Supreme Allied Command chose Thurleigh for their first major base concert in the United Kingdom. On Friday, July 14, playing on a stage which had been set up in one of the B-17 hangars, the orchestra received a mighty ovation when it opened with its theme of *Moonlight Serenade.* As the band followed with *In the Mood* and *Little Brown Jug,* Glenn knew from the tremendous reception that he had done the right thing in coming to England. During the interval, he told Colonel Ed Kirby from SHAEF headquarters; 'Making all the money in the band business could never make me feel this rich!'

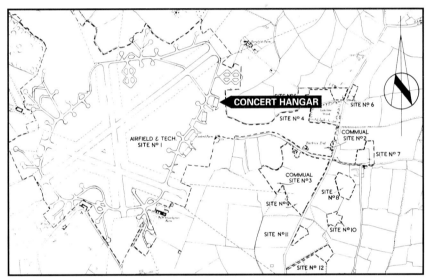

After the war, Thurleigh became a test centre for new projects undertaken by the Royal Aircraft Establishment. To facilitate this, the airfield was greatly extended and a new main runway now completely bisects the wartime technical site, completely expunging the site of the hangar where Glenn's first base concert was held. The airfield was closed in 1993.

127

Tibenham Station 124

Glenn Miller and the American Band of the AEF prepare for their concert at the 445th Bomb Group base at Tibenham on the afternoon of Friday, September 1, 1944.

NORFOLK

Tibenham airfield, also sometimes referred to as Tivetshall, lies some 13 miles south-west of Norwich and was the base of the Eighth Air Force's 445th Bomb Group. It was also the posting for over a year of Captain (later Colonel) James Stewart, the famous Hollywood film star, who was based here right through 1944. Jimmy was commander of the 703rd Bomb Squadron and he flew many combat missions from Tibenham in his B-24 Liberator *Nine Yanks and a Jerk*.

On the afternoon of Friday, September 1 — a day of no missions for the 445th — Major Glenn Miller and the dance band from the American Band of the AEF gave a concert in the No. 1 Hangar for an audience of 3,000. Afterwards, Miller and the band went on by road to nearby Thorpe Abbotts for another show that evening (see page 125).

Undoubtedly, James Stewart was present in the audience but who could imagine that ten years later he would play the lead part in the Hollywood film, *The Glenn Miller Story*.

On the base where the wartime T2 once stood, and in which the band played, a replacement hangar has been erected for use by the Norfolk Gliding Club.

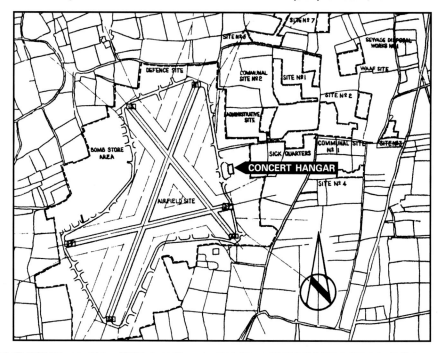

Twinwood Farm

BEDFORDSHIRE

The Royal Air Force airfield at Twinwood Farm, near the Bedfordshire village of Clapham, was built and opened in 1941. It was a satellite training airfield also used by night fighters and Pathfinder Moquitos, and was used as the main drop-off point by Miller's orchestra who were billeted three miles away in Bedford. Because of this, and the courtesy shown by the officers and staff at the airfield, the band gave them a one-hour concert on the warm sunny Sunday afternoon of August 27, 1944.

During the 50th anniversary year of 1994, this concert was repeated and re-enacted by the Glenn Miller (UK) Orchestra, directed by John Watson, as a tribute to the late Major Glenn Miller and his American Band of the AEF. Quite a few of the RAF personnel who were at the 1944 concert returned, together with many British fans from all over the United Kingdom.

Twinwood Farm was also the setting for the final act in Glenn Miller's life, as it was from here that he took off on his last fatal flight. The last view anyone saw of the musical genius would have been as his single-engined Norseman aircraft disappeared into the fog blanketing the airfield on Friday, December 15, 1944 (see page 136).

Above: **Glenn Miller directs as Sergeant Johnny Desmond sings at Twinwood Farm on Sunday, August 27, 1944. The 'stage' on which the band are playing is made up from a USAAF C-2 semi-trailer (in the background) and an RAF Eagle 2-ton trailer. The C2 was normally used by the band at their airfield concerts as it was readily available at American airbases. It was 50 feet long overall, with a 40ft × 8ft platform whereas the Eagle was only 24ft × 8ft.** *Below:* **The Glenn Miller (UK) Orchestra, conducted by John Watson, play for the 1994 audience on the afternoon of Sunday, August 28 during the special 50th anniversary concert on a modern platform!**

Sergeants Ray McKinley and 'Trigger' Alpert give their stage show for the RAF during the concert at Twinwood Farm held from 3.30 to 4.30 p.m. that sunny Sunday afternoon in 1944. Today, the runways have gone but the control tower and many of the outer buildings remain used for agricultural purposes. Needless to say, as this is the place where Glenn was last seen alive, over the years many thousands of his fans have made the pilgrimage to inspect what is left of the airfield.

Ghost stories about the control tower have sprung up, and it is now more than ever a shrine to the memory of one of the world's greatest bandleaders. For the 1994 concert, the trailer that John Watson's band used was set up on the same spot by the control tower, although it faced the opposite direction compared with the performance in 1944. Then, there was more space on the runway side; now, the audience sat roughly spread out between the band and the control tower.

The death of Glenn Miller was a tragic loss to popular music and, all the more so, to the morale of the Allied forces at that time. Fifty years later, on Thursday, December 15, 1994, at the exact time the aircraft took off, a Service of Remembrance was held on the very spot where the staff car had been parked. A United States Air Force chaplain read a prayer to the Lord of the Dance and the British Legion (Bedford) branch gave a special service. Also present was bandleader John Watson, from the Glenn Miller (UK) Orchestra and trumpeter Mike Lovatt who played the Last Post. The occasion was marked by the planting of a tree.

Left: Time for nostalgia during the 50th anniversary concert; time for remembrance a few months later *(right)*. The US Air Force provided an Honor Guard for the special service held on Thursday, December 15, 1994. The organisers, Gordon and Connie Richards, the UK representatives of the Eighth Air Force Historical Society, arranged for a scarlet oak to be planted where the wartime flagpole had stood and for three carnations to be air-dropped in memory of the three missing airmen.

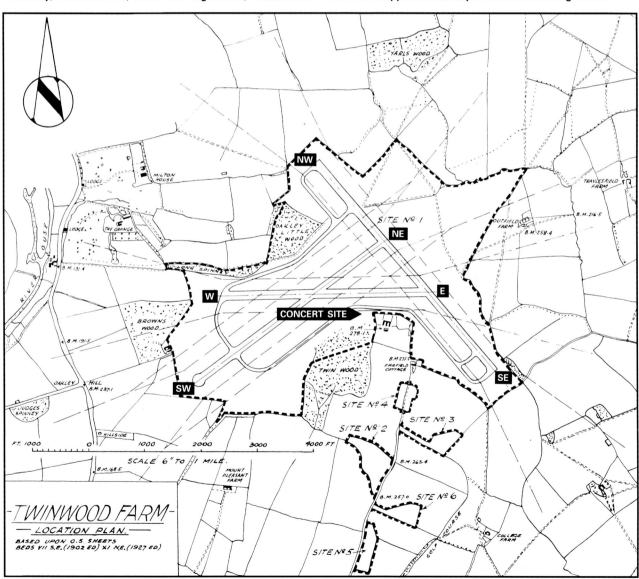

TWINWOOD FARM
— LOCATION PLAN. —
BASED UPON O.S. SHEETS
BEDS VII S.E.(1902 ED) XI N.E.(1927 ED)

Captain Glenn Miller and the American Band of the AEF perform a number featuring Ray McKinley on vocals outside Hangar No. 3 at Warton on Monday, August 14, 1944. In this case, the spectators get a good view of both sides of the band.

Warton Station 582

LANCASHIRE

Warton airfield, not far from the famous seaside resort of Blackpool, was opened in 1942 and became Base Air Depot No. 2 for the United States VIII Air Force Air Service Command. Warton and Burtonwood (see page 36) were the largest air base depots in the United Kingdom and were more like factories than airfields, with machine shops, service areas, warehouses and stores.

Late on the evening of Sunday, August 13, 1944, Glenn Miller and the dance band ensemble (better known as the Swing Shift) landed at Warton in two C-47 transports after flying over from Langford Lodge in Northern Ireland.

They spent the night at Warton and, the following afternoon between 4.00 and 5.00 p.m. in front of Hangar No. 3, Miller brought his 'Hunk 'O Home' concert to a huge audience of 10,000 service personnel stationed at the base. Also appearing was British singing star Dorothy Carless. The band opened with *In the Mood* and followed with *Chattanooga*

(RESTRICTED)

SPECIAL SERVICE

Vol. I. No. 22.   EDUCATION, ATHLETICS, ENTERTAINMENT.   Saturday, August 12th, 1944

GLENN MILLER AND BAND TO PLAY AT TECH AREA MONDAY

Capt. Glenn Miller and Orchestra will journey to this base in the next few days to give out with a swing session in front of Hanger No. 4, at approximately 16.00 hrs., MONDAY, AUGUST 14th.

This will be the only performance of this famous band, so let's turn out *en masse* for this Jam Session.

LIVERPOOL PHILHARMONIC CONCERT AT OPERA HOUSE

THANKS YANKS

The following letter has been received from the Blackpool Women's Voluntary Services for Civil Defence :

The appearance of the band at Warton was publicised in advance although they actually played outside Hangar No. 3, not No. 4 as advertised.

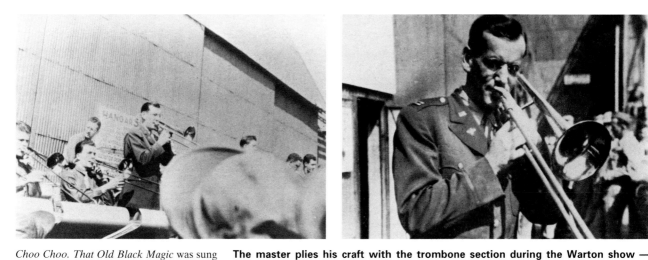

Choo Choo. That Old Black Magic was sung by Sergeant Johnny Desmond, the band played *Anvil Chorus,* and then Dorothy sang more hits. Instrumentals followed: *Tuxedo Junction, Rhapsody in Blue,* and *Stealing Apples* before Glenn turned the band over to drummer Sergeant Ray McKinley.

Miller and the band had dinner at the base before going sight-seeing in Blackpool. They stayed a second night at Warton and then, late on Tuesday morning (August 15), took off in two B-24s for Burtonwood.

The master plies his craft with the trombone section during the Warton show — wonderfully atmospheric snapshots which have surfaced in recent years.

Ray McKinley sings *Chattanooga Choo Choo* — the hit from *Sun Valley Serenade*.

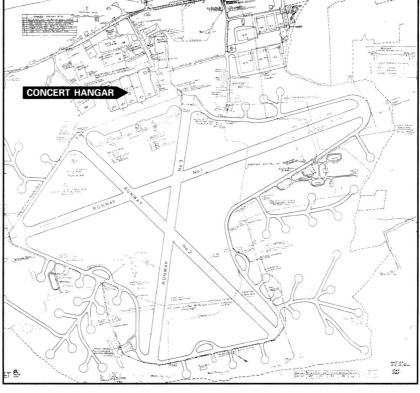

Today, Warton airfield belongs to British Aerospace and, although the hangars have been renewed, they stand in the same positions. Hangar No. 3 is now used for the manufacture of airframe components.

Glenn chats to the audience between numbers during the concert at Wattisham on Monday, July 24, 1944.

Wattisham Station 377

SUFFOLK

Wattisham, nine miles north-west of Ipswich, was completed in 1939 for the Royal Air Force which used the airfield until June 1942 when it was assigned to the United States Army Air Force. It was intended to upgrade the airfield with concrete runways for heavy bombers but this idea was dropped and it remained a fighter base with an associated air depot called Hitcham (Station 470) after the nearby village of that name. The airfield was occupied by the Eighth Air Force's 479th Fighter Group from May 1944.

On Monday afternoon, July 24, 1944, Glenn Miller and the Swing Shift (the dance band group) with Dorothy Carless gave an outdoor concert for a combined audience of 10,000 from the 479th Fighter Group and the supply depot. After the performance, Glenn Miller, Dorothy Carless and the rest of the band were entertained for dinner.

Wattisham remained an RAF base until July 1, 1993 when it was handed over to the Army Air Corps for accommodating units returning from Germany under the Options for Change programme. New works costing £50 million were put in hand, including the construction of two new hangars for the Gazelle and Lynx helicopters of 3 and 4 Regiments, with another huge complex for 7 Battalion, REME. *Above right:* **The concert was held beside one of the T2 hangars of the Hitcham air depot; unfortunately the hangar on the left of the picture was demolished in the 1980s when 'hardened' shelters were erected to protect dispersed aircraft from bomb blast.**

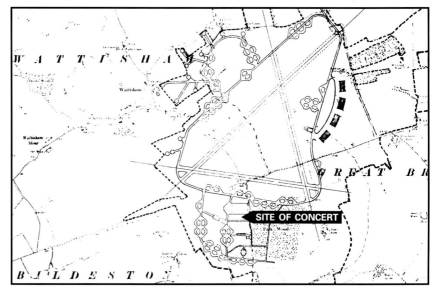

SITE OF CONCERT

Major Glenn Miller and the American Band of the AEF are introduced to the members of the 392nd Bomb Group at the beginning of the concert.

Wendling Station 118

NORFOLK

Wendling airfield, four miles west-north-west of East Dereham in Norfolk, was opened in 1943 and occupied by the 392nd Bomb Group which remained there with its B-24 Liberators until June 1945.

On the morning of Friday, August 25, 1944, the group's target was at Schwerin, east of Hamburg, but the crews had returned by 3.15 p.m. to hear Glenn and the American Band of the AEF. They played for 1¼ hours that afternoon in one of the B-24 hangars for 3,000 officers and enlisted personnel, after which the band was flown south to give a second concert at the B-17 bomber base at Knettishall in Suffolk (see page 62).

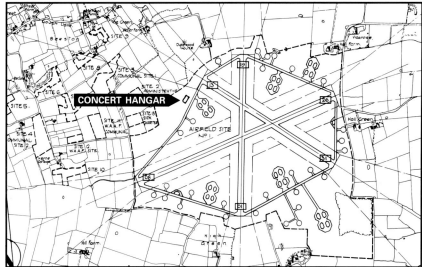

Wendling reverted to the RAF at the end of hostilities but was closed down in 1961. James Wiseman purchased that part of the airfield which included the hangar where the concert had been held although the T2 itself had already been dismantled. He reclaimed the land so well in the mid-1970s that today nothing remains to mark where it once stood, but James kindly broke off from his chores to drive out and position his tractor for us on the spot where the band had played in 1944.

No flight plan for Glenn Miller's final flight to France has ever been traced. Although Lieutenant Colonel Baessell was notionally travelling on official business for VIII Air Force Service Command, with an ultimate destination logged as Bordeaux, Miller was in effect hitching a ride to jump the queue waiting for a seat on the normal shuttle from Bovingdon to Paris. Baessell's pilot, Flight Officer John R. S. Morgan, was based at the 2nd Strategic Air Depot at Abbots Ripton which shared the adjacent airfield of Alconbury, and it was from there that he took off at 1325 hours on December 15, 1944 to pick up his two passengers from their usual airfield of Twinwood Farm, a 20-mile hop as the crow flies. Records show that with Baessell and Miller aboard, Morgan took off again at 1355 hours . . . never to be seen again.

SUPREME HEADQUARTERS
ALLIED EXPEDITIONARY FORCE
REAR HEADQUARTERS
APO 413

AG-201-AGF ÷ Miller,Alton G. (Off)   12 December 1944

SUBJECT : Orders.

TO : Major ALTON G. MILLER, 0606271 G-1 Division, Supreme HQ

1.   You will proceed by military aircraft (ATC) on or about
16 December 1944 from present station to SUPREME HQ,ARMY AG-TM
on the Continent to carry out the instructions of the A.C. of S
G1,SUPREME HQ AEF,and on completion thereof return to present
station.

2.   Travel by military aircraft is directed. Baggage allowance
limited to sixty-five (65) pounds.

By command of General Eisenhower

The Final Flight

On Monday, November 13, 1944, Major Glenn Miller was ordered to report to Supreme Headquarters Allied Expeditionary Force at Versailles, just outside Paris. The order had come from Lieutenant General Walter Bedell 'Beetle' Smith, General Eisenhower's Chief-of-Staff. Glenn was billeted from November 15 at the Hotel Crillon in Paris.

The meeting with General Smith lasted all of 30 seconds. Miller was asked to take command of the US Army Band but he told the General that he would not like that and they did not play his kind of music! The next four days were spent in talks with General Ray W. Barker, the SHAEF G-1, about bringing Glenn's American Band of the AEF over to Paris for a six-week tour of American bases and field hospitals beginning on or about December 15. The proposed tour would include entertaining front-line troops on leave in the French capital and include two special broadcasts on Christmas Day and New Year's Eve. Miller said he would leave the decision up to the band as they would have the task of pre-recording six weeks' programmes in advance, in addition to their normal broadcasting schedule.

Miller returned from Paris via the SHAEF shuttle to Bovingdon airfield in Hertfordshire on Saturday, November 18. Don Haynes picked up Miller from London and drove him back to the band's billets at Bedford. The next day, the members of the orchestra had the day off so Glenn had the opportunity to broach the idea of the French trip. All voted to go to Paris in December and, during the next few weeks, they made 83 reserve recordings for future use by the BBC.

On Saturday, November 25, Haynes flew to Paris at the suggestion of General Barker. He was to make arrangements for billets, transportation, mess facilities etc. In Paris, Haynes met his and Glenn's old friend from Milton Ernest Hall, Lieutenant Colonel Norman F. Baessell, who knew all the places to go including the top night spots. Haynes remained in Paris for a week and was scheduled to return to England from Orly airfield to Bovingdon on Friday, December 1; he finally got back to England at 11.25 a.m. the following morning.

A six-week tour of American bases in France was first proposed in November, the actual order detailing Glenn's journey to France being dated December 12. That evening, he and the band were appearing at the Queensbury All Services Club (see page 85); it was to be his last public appearance. (Note: Miller's serial number typed on the order is incorrect; it should be 0505273. Supreme Headquarters (SHAEF Main) had been located at Versailles, south-west of Paris, since mid-September.)

On the evening of Tuesday, December 12, Glenn gave his last live broadcast in the United Kingdom from the Queensbury All Services Club in Old Compton Street, in the heart of London's Soho, when Irish-American singer Morton Downey was the special guest.

The weather at the time was terrible, with thick, foggy conditions throughout England and Don Haynes noted in his diary that 'even the conductors of the red double-decked buses walked in front with flashlights'. Glenn stayed overnight at his suite at the Mount Royal Hotel, while the orchestra returned to Bedford that evening.

Haynes had told Miller several days before that he had overlooked one point while in France: the transportation from Orly airfield into Paris. Miller told Haynes as he wanted to sort this out personally, he would go instead of Haynes, who already had orders to fly to Paris on or about December 14, a fact which he pointed out to his boss. 'Uncut the orders and have them changed', was Miller's reply. Haynes went straight to SHAEF at Bushy Park the very next day and did just that. Thus, the course of events on the fate of Glenn Miller was slowly falling into place.

Haynes returned to Bedford and spent Wednesday at the American Red Cross Club in Goldington Road and at Milton Ernest Hall. The same day, BBC producer Cecil Madden dropped into the Mount Royal to see Glenn. He told him: 'Make sure the boats they send you on are seaworthy'. When Madden learned that Miller was intending to fly, he tried in vain to talk him out of going but Glenn told him a white lie about having to go to a special function in Paris, and that as he had promised to attend, he had to fly over. The band would follow in transport aircraft.

The next day, Thursday, December 14, while Haynes was having lunch with Baessell at the Officers' Club at Milton Ernest, Miller telephoned Haynes. Glenn explained he had tried in vain to get a flight out via the shuttle at Bovingdon, but nothing was leaving due to the weather and that, in any case, there would be a week's backlog to clear before he would be allocated a flight. Baessell overheard the conversation and asked to speak to Miller. He said that he had already arranged to go to Paris by air the next day from the RAF airfield at Twinwood Farm, three miles north of Bedford, and he invited Miller to join him. The invitation was accepted with alacrity and Haynes drove to London to bring Miller back to Bedford.

That evening, Miller, Haynes and Baessell had dinner together at Milton Ernest Officers' Club. They then played a few hands of poker with Major William Koch and Warrant Officer Neal Earlywine (both stationed at Milton Ernest Hall). Before they left for their quarters in Goldington Road, Baessell told Miller they would be leaving on a 9 a.m. flight the following morning.

Next morning, Bedford was fogged in. At 8.20 a.m., Haynes checked with Baessell by telephone who said that the fog was due to lift at about noon and that he anticipated that they would be leaving for Paris shortly after lunch. After a leisurely breakfast, Miller and Haynes drove to the enlisted men's billets in Ashburnham Road to see if everything was ready for the move to Paris the next day (December 16). Bass player, 'Trigger' Alpert, had received three Christmas packages from his wife, but as the band could only take one parcel each to France, Glenn offered to take the other two with him and hand them over in Paris. From there, Miller and Haynes drove to Milton Ernest Hall to meet up with Baessell.

Arriving at the HQ, Baessell told them he had just talked on the telephone with their pilot, Flight Officer John R. S. 'Nipper' Morgan of the 35th Air Depot at Abbots Ripton. Morgan told him the weather was improving and that he would know shortly after noon if he would get clearance to take off. Haynes took it that Morgan was taking off from Abbots Ripton but this strategic air depot had no separate airfield and shared the adjacent bomber field at Alconbury. So, a twisted fact comes into the story at this point which, over the years, would lead some authors and even the US Air Force itself to believe that the ill-fated UC-64-A Norseman took off from an airfield named Abbots Ripton. No trace of clearance at this base has ever been found and, of course, none is ever likely to be, as Morgan's flight plan would have been logged at Alconbury!

After landing to collect his passengers waiting at Twinwood Farm, Morgan's planned route was most probably west before turning south to pass to the west of Greater London. The flight path would then have crossed the River Thames, leaving England at Beachy Head and out over the Channel towards northern France and then straight to the Ninth Air Force airfield at Villacoublay (A-42), ten miles south-west of Paris. No mention was made of another landing at Bovingdon or anywhere else in the United Kingdom.

Lieutenant Colonel Norman F. Baessell is pictured here in the grounds of the VIII Air Force Service Command HQ at Milton Ernest in 1944. Baessell was responsible for establishing advanced air depots on the Continent to service damaged aircraft there rather than return them to the UK. He made frequent flights to France and Belgium and had achieved somewhat of a reputation for flying in conditions less than ideal.

During lunch at Milton Ernest Hall, Baessell received another telephone call from Morgan saying that he had just received clearance and he would pick them up at Twinwood Farm within the hour.

Major Koch and Warrant Officer Earlywine walked out to the staff car to see them off. En route, Haynes drove first to the house of General Donald Goodrich who was ill in bed, having been relieved of his command and replaced by Colonel James F. Early on December 5. Miller and Haynes remained outside in the vehicle and, after about ten minutes, Baessell returned to the car.

Milton Ernest Hall has already featured in an earlier chapter; now it becomes the 'set' for the opening scene in the tragedy of Friday, December 15. Here it was that the arrangements for the fatal flight were finalised, and here it was that Miller enjoyed his last meal before walking across this courtyard *(left)* to exit from this gateway *(above)* to turn onto the A6 trunk road.

Colonel Baessell first called in to see his former chief, Brigadier General Donald Goodrich, bedridden in his house called 'The Bury' just across the river at Oakley. Don Haynes then retraced his route and crossed the A6 to enter Twinwood Farm by the

rear entrance (see overleaf) passing Brownswood Farm (left). He parked outside the control tower (right) while Baessell entered the doorway on the left to check on Morgan's arrival. They did not have long to wait.

Ten minutes later they drove into the RAF station at Twinwood Farm and sat in the staff car smoking and talking. The heavy rain had eased off into a steady drizzle with a cloud base of 200 feet. Baessell left the car and reported to the control tower. Upon his return, he said that Morgan had already taken off from Alconbury and would therefore be arriving any minute. Miller got out of the smoke-filled car and was joined by Baessell and Haynes. Haynes walked to

the control tower and noted that the thermometer there registered 34 degrees Fahrenheit. Miller had just quipped that Morgan would not find the field as even the birds were grounded when they then heard the steady drone of an aircraft engine. Hidden by the overcast, Morgan flew over the field. The aircraft turned and then appeared through the cloud over the centre of the airfield, circled once again and then landed.

No photographs were taken on that fateful Friday; indeed, why should they because the departure was a low-key affair with only Don Haynes present to see Glenn off. Of all the pictures which came our way during the production of this book, the one below would seem to be the most appropriate to include

at this point. Although it is one of those from the Burtonwood sequence on August 15 (see pages 36 and 37), it seems to depict a certain quality in the relationship between Haynes and Miller; one must just imagine the fog and overcoats of the final scene played out precisely four months later.

Three days before I was to leave, and precede the band by another couple of days, Glenn said that he felt he would go on ahead and that I would bring the band over afterwards. Glenn gave the impression that he had a lot of things to do and a very short space of time as though he did not have enough time to do all the things that he had planned to do. This was not unlike him, overseas, because he would make split-second decisions and was seldom ever wrong. So I said 'Well Glenn, I have orders cut to precede the band to the Continent,' and he said in his unmilitary jargon: 'Well uncut 'em and get some cut for me!' Which was done but I do have a funny feeling he went on a plane trip that I had arranged with Colonel Baessell and Flight Officer Morgan in my place. And I can't help but feel that I'm on a sort of rain-check, as it were.

The last time I saw Glenn was when I drove he and Colonel Baessell out to a Beaufighter base, about three miles outside of Bedford, England — that's in the midlands of England about 52 miles north of London. It was a cold, rainy, foggy afternoon which is typical of English weather — they have summer over there on a Wednesday afternoon in July. We waited for the plane that was to pick them up coming from another base, piloted by a wonderful guy, a Flight Officer Morgan, with whom I had flown all over the European Theater.

We didn't think he'd find the field; he finally did with his instrument flying and came down and landed on the runway and didn't even set the motor off and I drove the staff car out to the runway and put Glenn and Colonel Baessell on the plane. That was the last time I saw him. As Glenn got on the plane or stepped on the step to get into this C-64 Norseman — it was a singled-engine plane — he gathered his trench coat about him to ward off the chilling mist and, before closing the door of the ship, he glanced up at the horrible weather and he said: 'Haynsie. Even the birds are grounded today!'

DON HAYNES,
INTERVIEW WITH ANDY WILLIAMS, 1958

The tower at Twinwood Farm is remarkably preserved . . .

Baessell, Miller and Haynes got back into the car and Haynes drove to the end of the runway to the waiting plane which turned out to be a single-engined, Canadian-built Noordwyn Norseman UC-64-A, serial number 44-70285. Morgan opened the door of the plane and apologised for being late. He explained he had run into some heavy squalls

Above: Flight Officer John R. S. Morgan was officially an Assistant Engineer Officer whose job it was to ferry aircraft spare parts and, if necessary, personnel. Although he had experience on a variety of aircraft types, he was not a combat pilot and is reported to have been inexperienced in instrument flying. *Below:* This is the actual aircraft he used on December 15 — a UC-64-A Norseman, serial number 44-70285, pictured at Alconbury sometime during the autumn of 1944 with one of the ground crew, Staff Sergeant Art Nanas.

POST-WAR ROAD

. . . with many of the original fittings still to be seen . . . including this door to the vitally-important Met Office.

but that the weather was supposed to be clearing over the Continent. Colonel Baessell handed his B-4 bag to Morgan and went back to the staff car for a case of empty champagne bottles he was taking with him (bottles were scarce in Paris and empty bottles had to be returned in order to purchase more champagne). Haynes tossed Miller's bag into the open cabin door. Baessell then climbed into the co-pilot's seat, while Miller seated himself in a bucket seat directly behind, facing the side of the plane. Haynes closed the door and secured the latch and stepped away. At 1.55 p.m. the aircraft took off on the westward-facing runway and disappeared into the low overcast.

CONTROL TOWER ►

◄ MAIN ENTRANCE

◄ REAR ENTRANCE

BROWNSWOOD FARM ►

FROM A6

According to Don Haynes, the only eyewitness to the departure, the Norseman remained on the runway after it had touched down and he drove out to meet it. Today, the concrete has been removed but we asked our pilot to come down low over the line of the old E-W runway on which Morgan had landed (see plan page 131). We then took this shot looking back to the airfield from the direction that Glenn would have last seen it as they disappeared into the overcast.

The final destination of the flight was Bordeaux, with one stop en route at Villacoublay to allow Miller to get off. When Haynes and the rest of the orchestra flew into Orly on Monday (18th), to find neither transport to meet them nor Glenn Miller to greet them, only then did they discover that his aircraft had never arrived.

During the week before Christmas, SHAEF and the US Air Force Service Command HQ at Milton Ernest checked every possible report and airfield in the United Kingdom and all those throughout Allied-held Europe. No trace of the Norseman could be found and there was only one report of a light aircraft flying out over the Sussex coast heading for France on December 15. However, no trace could be found of it ever reaching the French coast.

On Christmas Eve, Glenn's wife Helen was informed of the tragic loss of her husband, and Don Haynes told the orchestra on Christmas morning. Later that day, the BBC announced that Major Glenn Miller had been reported missing on flight from England to France some ten days previously. Without their leader, the band, directed by Sergeant Jerry Gray, then went ahead with the Christmas Day broadcast from the Olympia Theatre in Paris on a direct line hook up with England and the USA.

Many ideas have been put forward over the years about the fate of the aircraft and Glenn Miller on that Friday afternoon. Some are so fanciful that they are not even worth considering, most of the wild theories appearing to be put forward by those seeking weird publicity for their own ends. This hurts Glenn's family, which, over the years, has had to suffer terrible lies and untruths. I know what Glenn's two children, Steve and Jonnie, saw happening to their mother, as I experienced more or less the same thing with my mother who lost her only brother (also in 1944) somewhere in the China seas. Glenn's wife went through hell, hoping upon hope that Glenn would suddenly turn up. This never happened, and Helen Miller died in 1966.

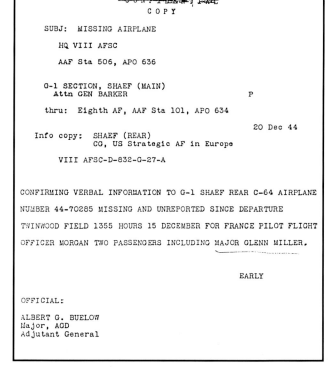

CONFIDENTIAL
COPY

SUBJ: MISSING AIRPLANE

  HQ VIII AFSC

  AAF Sta 506, APO 636

G-1 SECTION, SHAEF (MAIN)
  Attn GEN BARKER   P

  thru: Eighth AF, AAF Sta 101, APO 634

                              20 Dec 44
  Info copy: SHAEF (REAR)
             CG, US Strategic AF in Europe

  VIII AFSC-D-832-G-27-A

CONFIRMING VERBAL INFORMATION TO G-1 SHAEF REAR C-64 AIRPLANE
NUMBER 44-70285 MISSING AND UNREPORTED SINCE DEPARTURE
TWINWOOD FIELD 1355 HOURS 15 DECEMBER FOR FRANCE PILOT FLIGHT
OFFICER MORGAN TWO PASSENGERS INCLUDING MAJOR GLENN MILLER.

                           EARLY

OFFICIAL:

ALBERT G. BUELOW
Major, AGD
Adjutant General

This message was sent to General Ray Barker (the SHAEF G-1) from the new commanding officer of VIII Air Force Service Command, Colonel James F. Early, the following Wednesday.

When Haynes arrived in Paris, he asked the newspaper chief, William Randolph Hearst, to ask the Allied Press to seek out any news of Glenn. Needless to say they drew a blank. Haynes followed up every possible lead but nothing ever came to light from that day to this. However, we are still bombarded with fanciful stories which do more harm than good, like the one about Glenn being in a fight in a brothel. If he did reach Paris safely, what happened to the aircraft, its pilot and Colonel Baessell?

So what did happen to the plane and its three occupants? The most credible answer is that it simply came down in the Channel. The US Air Force have always maintained that it iced up and fell like a stone. During the Eighth Air Force inquiry held on January 20, 1945, which Haynes attended, it was reported that if this had happened, the wings would have detached and floated for up to 18 hours after the crash. Almost certainly though, even if the occupants had got out, they would not have lasted long in the freezing water.

AG 201-AGF-Miller, Alton Glenn (Off)

PAIN, APO 757
22 December 1944

SUBJECT: Report of Missing Personnel.

TO : Commanding General, European Theater of Operations, U. S. Army, APO 887.

1. It is reported that on 15 December 1944 Major Alton Glenn Miller, O-505273, AC, Army Air Force Band (Special), Headquarters Command, Supreme Headquarters AEF, departed from an airport in England enroute to Paris, France, in an Eighth Air Force Service Command airplane (C-64) piloted by a Flight Officer Morgan. There was one (1) additional passenger on this plane - a Lieutenant Colonel Baessel of the Eighth Air Force. Major Miller was taken to the air field by an officer of the Army Air Force Band who witnessed the take-off. No trace of this plane can be found and this headquarters has been advised by the Eighth Air Force Service Command that this airplane is considered missing. Likewise, Major Miller is considered to be missing.

2. It is requested that an immediate radio casualty report be rendered to the War Department on Major Miller, and the War Department be advised that in view of the circumstances set forth in paragraph 4 below, it is considered highly desirable that this information be released to the press here at 1800A hours, 24 December, and that the War Department should confirm to your headquarters the next of kin has been notified prior to that time.

3. The next of kin of Major Miller is Mrs. Helen D. Miller (wife), Cotswold Apartments, Byrne Lane, Tenafly, New Jersey, telephone, Englewood 3-7311.

4. A Christmas Day broadcast has been scheduled which will be released to the United States. Major Miller was to have participated in this program. It is thought considerable publicity has been given to this broadcast in the United States.

For the Supreme Commander:

T. J. DAVIS,
Brigadier General,
Adjutant General.

8.-1163

RECEIVED

CONFIDENTIAL

Not hearing anything to the contrary, Don Haynes and the rest of the members of the band expected Glenn to be at the airport in Paris to greet them on Monday morning according to plan. When he was not there, it was assumed that he had been held up somewhere and enquiries were set in motion. However, by Friday, when there was still no news of either the aircraft or its occupants, a formal report to General Eisenhower, the Supreme Commander, could no longer be delayed.

An awkward situation now presented itself. Not wishing to announce the news that Glenn Miller was definitely dead, in case he suddenly turned up, yet well aware that a live broadcast had already been scheduled for Christmas Day, the press release was held up for as long as possible.

Another explanation put forward in the 1980s is that the plane got lost and strayed into a jettison zone and that a returning bomber on an aborted mission released its bombs above the Norseman. On the day in question, there were RAF Lancasters returning shortly after midday from an aborted raid, and they had been instructed to get rid of their bombs in mid-Channel, more or less on the route that Morgan would have taken, but the time that the Norseman might have reached the spot compared to when the aircraft were dropping their bombs is nearly an hour adrift. The jettison theory is also confused with another Norseman lost that day which is reported to have departed from Grove airfield (near Oxford — see page 48) about the same time, also bound for France.

There are simple explanations for several inaccuracies in the various wartime reports yet some authors deliberately try to read subterfuge into any discrepancy. What sense would there be to deliberately obscure the truth concerning Glenn's death? The very fact that some of the contemporary documents are at variance with each other surely adds *more* credence to their authenticity, not less? Had there been any official attempt at a 'cover up', as several authors have claimed, one would expect a more coherant set of paperwork to have been produced.

In a nutshell, the flight was unwise in the prevailing weather conditions and the pilot has been said to be wanting in his experience of instrument flying. The aircraft was not equipped to deal with the icing which would almost certainly have been encountered and, because of the cloud base, the single-engined machine would have had to cross the Channel at an altitude that would preclude any recovery following engine failure.

PUBLIC RELATIONS DIVISION

S H A E F

_____

24 Dec. 1944

Memo to: Capt Wade
Information Room

Here is the release on Glenn Miller, with the embargo of 1800 hours tonight.

Colonel Dupuy merely wants a factual announcement that he is missing. However, he also wants a statment added to the effect that "no members of his band were with him." Or something very much like that.

Capt. Cosgrove.

THIS CORRESPONDENCE MUST BE RETURNED. COLONEL DUPUY DOES NOT HAVE TO SEE THE RELEASE BEFORE IT GOES OUT.

Done.

Signature 1150
24 Dec 44
P.V.W.

8 1159

REF NO. 605

**Supreme Headquarters
ALLIED EXPEDITIONARY FORCE
Public Relations Division**

FOR RELEASE AT   24 December 1944
1800 HOURS

Major Alton Glenn Miller, director of the famous United States Army Air Force band which has been playing in Paris is reported missing while on a flight from England to Paris. The plane in which he was a passenger left England on December 15 and no trace of it has been found since its take-off.

Major Miller, one of the outstanding orchestra leaders in the United States, lived at Tenafly, New Jersey, where his wife presently resides.

No members of Major Miller's band were with him on the missing plane.

Beyond our sight yet never to be forgotten. A group of Miller fans seek out his name, carved in stone on the Wall of the

Missing at the American Military Cemetery at Madingley, west of Cambridge.

On Saturday, December 15, 1945, one year after Major Glenn Miller, Lieutenant Colonel Norman Baessell and the pilot, Flight Officer John Morgan, took off, the United States Army Air Force officially declared them dead, with the explanation that they died with no known grave somewhere in the English Channel. Today, the names of all three are memorialised on the Wall of the Missing at the American Military Cemetery at Madingley, near Cambridge.

Today, whenever and wherever the Glenn Miller sound is heard, to those who remember, it revives like nothing else the bitter-sweet memories of the Second World War. The colours may fade but his music will live on . . . for ever.

The Films

On Thursday, September 14, 1944, Major Glenn Miller recorded a special interview with Vernon Harris of the BBC at Broadcasting House in London. This interview was inserted into the programme *Here's Wishing You Well*, aimed at hospitals. The segment known as the 'Wishing Well' was aired by the BBC seven days later on Thursday, September 21 and, during the course of the interview (which has been preserved), Harris asked about the British reaction to the American Band of the AEF. 'From a personal standpoint it's been really wonderful', said Glenn. 'The Tommies we have played for have made us feel right at home and we were surprised to find that the British youngsters in the service are well educated to our American style of music.' When Harris pointed out: 'Well, don't forget your records got here before you did', Glenn replied: 'Well I hadn't thought of that.'

Not only had the records reached Britain before Miller, but both the British armed forces and the general public had seen Glenn and heard his famous sound during his two movies, *Sun Valley Serenade* (1941) and *Orchestra Wives* (1942). Both films were made by 20th Century Fox and *Sun Valley Serenade*, made in the spring of 1941 in Hollywood, was nominated that year for three Oscars: cinematography, scoring of a musical picture, and the best song. That song, *Chattanooga Choo Choo*, as recorded and issued by Glenn Miller, will remain a standard for all time, the Glenn Miller orchestra being awarded the first Gold Record in history for sales of over one million copies.

The two films were often shown by the Special Services Division of the United States War Department at army camps, hospitals, depot's and airfields. They were even shown in rest areas just behind the front lines.

Both films are still very popular and have been shown on television both here in Britain and in the USA. They were released on videocassette by Fox Video in 1995.

Sun Valley Serenade, which basically tells the story of the band manager (Milton Berle) at an Idaho resort taking care of a Norwegian refugee (Sonja Henie), is described as a 'simple-minded musical which still pleases because of the talent involved'. *Above:* The film was made by 20th Century Fox in Hollywood in April-May 1941, this shot showing Glenn Miller, who plays 'Phil Corey' in the film (the band is called the 'Dartmouth Troubadours') on trombone, with John Payne on the piano in the hotel lobby. The tune: *In the Mood. Below:* Apart from Glenn, seen here with Milton Berle in the fur coat and Lynn Bari, the film featured Joan Davis, Dorothy Dandridge and the Nicholas Brothers.

In *Orchestra Wives*, 'a fresh and lively musical, full of first-class music', a small-town girl (Ann Rutherford) marries the singer (George Montgomery) of a travelling swing band led by 'Gene Morrison', alias Glenn Miller. Stars pictured *(right)* are (L-R): Frank Orth, Lynn Bari, Cesar Romero, Glenn Miller, Marion Hutton (the regular vocalist with his band), George Montgomery, Jackie Gleason, Ray Eberle (the regular singer), with other members of the band in the background.

Glenn Miller and his band on the Hollywood sound stage during the making of *Orchestra Wives* in the spring of 1942. The film had its premiere in Britain at the London Pavilion and the Regal Marble Arch on January 29, 1943. When Glenn and his orchestra toured Britain in the summer of 1944, they often featured hits like *Chattanooga Choo Choo* by popular demand from his audiences who had seen his two films. British guest stars like Doreen Villiers and Paula Green (who broadcast with Glenn on August 24 and September 14) sang hits from the movies. Doreen Villiers song was *That's Sabotage* and Paula Green sang the beautiful *At Last*. Both came from *Orchestra Wives*, but *That's Sabotage* was cut from the released film, although it has been stated that the only country to see the song being sung by Marion Hutton was Canada.

The Glenn Miller Story, released in 1954, was a huge box office hit, reviewed as a 'competent musical heartwarmer with a well-cast star and successful reproduction of the Miller sound'. Valentine Davies and Oscar Brodney cleverly scripted Glenn's life for the screen, always a difficult job at a time when films only ran to 90 minutes. (*The Glenn Miller Story* overran and ended up at 116 minutes.) It was undoubtedly James Stewart's portrayal that really brought the character to life, the actor's service in the Eighth Air Force, and personal attendance at Miller airfield concerts, undoubtedly helping him to accurately create the part. *Right:* The sequence where 'Miller' jazzes up the march past at a US Army Air Force base in the USA (filmed at Lowry AFB, Denver, Colorado) was fine for this exterior shot although the interior of a States-side hangar *(below)* can hardly double for a British wartime T2. Francis Langford, who sings *Chattanooga Choo Choo* at this concert, was actually part of Bob Hope's show during the war, although the Modernaires accompanying her had performed with the Miller band in 1941.

In 1946, the year the Glenn Miller Orchestra, directed by Tex Beneke was formed, a Hollywood film company came up with the idea of making a movie on the life of the late Major Glenn Miller. By 1948 the proposal had been dropped but in 1953 Universal Pictures picked up on it again, featuring James Stewart in the title rôle. Stewart, who had served in the Eighth Air Force in England, was the ideal choice for he had seen Glenn Miller perform in England on August 18, 1944 at Attlebridge and, most probably, at Tibenham on September 1.

Although *The Glenn Miller Story* incorrectly portrayed certain events, and included the usual amount of poetic licence, the love story between Glenn and Helen, played by June Allyson, was very true to life. However, the details about Glenn's move to England before D-Day were wrong although the film did capture the spirit of the moment, like the concert in a packed hangar, with airmen and ground crews sitting on a B-17 Flying Fortress.

The use of well-known musicians was an added bonus. Front (L-R): James 'Trummy' Young (trombone); William 'Cozy' Cole (drums); Barney Bigard (clarinet) and Arvell Shaw (bass). Rear: Ben Pollack (drums); Gene Krupa (drums); Louis Armstrong (trumpet and vocals); James Stewart with Joe Yukl who played Miller's trombone solos; and Marty Napoleon (piano).

The likeness of Stewart with Miller's widely-known publicity shot taken in 1940 was uncanny.

Funnily enough, the scene nobody believed was the V1 flying bomb approaching during the outdoor concert but this really did take place, although perhaps not as dramatically as portrayed in the film. It happened at the Bentley Priory concert on August 16, 1944, but in the film the building shown looks more like Wycombe Abbey.

This scene was filmed outside Kittredge Castle at 6925 East 8th Avenue in Denver, Colorado. At the time, it was in use as the Mary E. Holland Children's Home and several of its children had bit-parts in the film. It was demolished in 1955.

Right: 'Hey, it's kind of soupy isn't it?' The film shows Glenn Miller and Don Haynes (played by Charles Drake, left) greeting Norman Baessell (Steve Pendleton) at the door of the Norseman whereas, in reality, all three arrived at Twinwood Farm together. *Below:* 'As some of you might know, Major Glenn Miller is not with us today. But in his absence, we shall do this programme exactly as he had planned it.' Filmed on the 1943 *Phantom of the Opera* set at the Universal Studios, this scene depicting Don Haynes on the stage of the Olympia Theatre in Paris was cut from the film when released. Instead, the final scene shows June Allyson (playing Helen Miller) listening to the Christmas Day broadcast from Paris in her home in Tenafly, New Jersey, and the band opening with *Little Brown Jug*. However, this is an over-simplification of what really happened. All three bands of the AEF took part in the programme, the British and Canadian playing at the Queensbury All Services Club in London. And Don Haynes actually made his announcement before the finale after which Mel Powell tinkled the notes of the AEF signature tune, *Oranges and Lemons*, which the American band then picked up.

Perhaps the most memorable scene in the film is the take-off by Miller on his final flight, which brought the legend even more to light.

The final scene was also true to life except for the storyline about the *Little Brown Jug* which had already been recorded by Glenn and his civilian band back in 1939. Nevertheless, *The Glenn Miller Story* is, without doubt, a very good bio-pic even by Hollywood standards and the music content was so good that it led directly to the formation of the New Glenn Miller Orchestra under Ray McKinley in 1956.

. . . and the band played on. In fine tradition, and in honour of its absent leader — still officially listed as missing — the orchestra remained on the Continent until August 1945 when it returned direct to the States. This particular concert was held in Nuremburg, Germany, on July 1, 1945. Don Haynes wrote in his diary that they 'played Nuremburg Stadium today to 40,000 screaming and cheering GIs. This same stadium was the scene of many of Adolf Hitler's gatherings, where he displayed the strength of the Nazi Party amid banner-waving crowds of sympathizers.' Unfortunately, Don Haynes was misinformed as the picture was taken in the old football stadium whereas Hitler used the Zepplinweise or the Luitpoldhain for his rallies. Here, Sergeant Ray McKinley leads the band; he shared conducting duties with Sergeant Jerry Gray after Glenn's death.

The Band Plays On

On August 12, 1945, Major Glenn Miller's American Band of the AEF returned home to the USA. After 13 months' service in Europe, and minus their missing leader, they had continued with their radio broadcasts but now the war was over and slowly the musicians were returned to civilian life.

During late 1945, Captain Don Haynes (he was promoted in July 1945) began talks with Glenn's widow, Helen, about reforming the Glenn Miller Orchestra as they both felt that Glenn would not have stood still. First, they got together as many of the former musicians who had been with Glenn overseas from the service outfit, plus odd members of the pre-war orchestra. The leadership was offered to Ray McKinley, who had been with the wartime orchestra from 1943 until 1945, but Ray had other ideas so they brought in former civilian band musician, tenor saxophonist, Gordon 'Tex' Beneke, who had spent the war in the US Navy leading a small service band in the USA. So from February 1946, Tex led the official Glenn Miller Orchestra, plus singers. However, in 1950, after several rows with the Miller Estate, Tex went his own way, but he has led a Glenn Miller sounding band ever since.

Between 1950 and 1956, there were also two very good imitators in the USA, one being led by the former arranger with both Glenn's civilian band and the orchestra that toured England, Jerry Gray. The second, Ralph Flanagan, had no connection with Miller but was a musician who had only heard Glenn in his heyday.

After the outstanding success of the Universal film *The Glenn Miller Story* in 1954/55, the Miller Estate reformed a New Glenn Miller Orchestra under the direction of Ray McKinley. Ray, of course, knew the Miller music well, having served with the wartime band from 1943 until 1945, and he also introduced quite a few modern tunes in the same style. The Ray McKinley-led orchestra opened in New York City in 1956, and lasted until 1965. Ray even brought the orchestra to Britain early in 1958 and performed in London's West End and at US Air Force bases. When Ray quit the band in 1965 for a quieter life and to spend more time with his family, the orchestra was taken over by Buddy DeFranco who had been with Tommy Dorsey just before his death.

In the early 1970s, the Glenn Miller band's style changed. Although they still recorded Miller music, it was played in Herb Alpert style and, inevitably, it did not find favour. This directly led to the formation of one of the top Miller-style orchestras of all time by trumpet player, Syd Lawrence. Syd was discovered performing Miller music true to the original in a Manchester pub in 1969 and his band was a success story from the word go, proving to be just what the British public wanted to see and hear.

Meanwhile, back in the USA, Buddy DeFranco had been replaced in 1975 as leader of the Glenn Miller Orchestra by trombone player Buddy Morrow but, later that same year, he was replaced by Jimmy Henderson. Jimmy spent six years as the leader of the official orchestra before being replaced in 1981 by Larry O'Brien who had been lead trombonist and soloist with the Tommy Dorsey band from 1962. Larry was superceded by Dick Gerhart in 1983.

Tex Beneke's orchestra, which performed in the immediate post-war years as the official Glenn Miller orchestra, was the nearest to duplicate the 40-piece wartime band. The unique Miller sound was originally produced with 22 strings and an equal number of brass instruments, but financial constraints limit latter-day orchestras to less than 20 musicians.

The official Glenn Miller orchestra in the United States has undergone several changes since Tex quit in 1950. The New Glenn Miller Orchestra was reformed in 1956 in response to the revival of interest following the release of *The Glenn Miller Story*, Buddy DeFranco taking over from Ray McKinley in 1965. Ten years later, Buddy was replaced as leader for a short time by Buddy Morrow before Jimmy Henderson was brought in. Jimmy led the band from 1975 to 1981 when Larry O'Brien took over. Dick Gerhart replaced him from 1983 to 1988 when Larry returned to once again lead the band. *Above:* This concert was staged in Glenn's home town, Clarinda, Iowa, by the Glenn Miller Birthplace Society in June 1995.

In Britain, it was Syd Lawrence who was instrumental in first creating a band to play in the Miller style. Although not officially-recognised by the copyright-owners in the USA as an official Glenn Miller orchestra, Syd left the BBC Northern Dance Orchestra after a stay of 15 years to form his own band in 1969 to begin touring the country on a full-time basis. He brought his orchestra to the Royal Festival Hall later that year for the first of the annual Glenn Miller Anniversary Concerts. With Syd now in retirement, the orchestra is led today by his former pianist and musical arranger, Bryan Pendleton. Before his death in August 1995, Alan Dell, the BBC's 'Mr Big Band', wrote of the orchestra: 'A quarter of a century is a long time for any big band to exist continuously and Syd's has outstripped many a famous name of the past both in Britain and America and what's more it has been done in the adverse climate of the Rock and Roll age. But quality and dedication will always have the respect it's due and how honourably the Syd Lawrence Orchestra has earned it and how much has been due to the loyal appreciation of its ever widening audience.'

Over in England, another Miller band was now beginning to take off: the Herb Miller Orchestra. Herb was Glenn's younger brother and was dedicated to putting together a super band to follow in his famous brother's footsteps. Herb first came to England in 1978 as a guest trumpet star with an ill-fated Ray Shields band. (Ray played what he called Glenn Miller music, but it was highly slanted towards the style of Count Basie.) Herb Miller returned to Britain in mid-1981 with one of his sons, John, and between them they began putting an orchestra together. Like most bands, the Herb Miller Orchestra struggled at first but by the mid-1980s it was an out and out success. Herb Miller died in East Dulwich Hospital on September 30, 1987, whereupon John took over. This band continues to keep the legend alive to this day.

The only band with a direct family link to Glenn Miller is the Herb Miller Orchestra formed in Britain by Glenn's younger brother in the 1980s. Although legal reasons preclude it claiming to be an 'official' Glenn Miller orchestra, it was chosen to play the memorable concert at Wycombe Abbey on July 24, 1988 when extra musicians were hired for the day to make up an equivalent-sized orchestra to recreate the wartime concert held on the same spot in July 1944 (see page 54). Since Herb died in September 1987, the band has been led by his son, John, who kindly contributed the foreword to this book.

Just after Herb Miller died, his band manager, John Watson, pulled away to form the British officially-led orchestra called The Glenn Miller (UK) Orchestra. Its start was also set with trials but today it, too, is beaming with success.

In the USA, the Glenn Miller Orchestra had also changed leaders again, Dick Gerhart being replaced by Larry O'Brien who had left the band back in 1981.

So today in the mid-1990s, we have two official Glenn Miller orchestras: one in the United States led by Larry O'Brien and the other in the United Kingdom by John Watson. Both are authorised to use the Miller music library and Glenn's name and, like the man they set out to remember, they have performed in some very historic places connected with Glenn's wartime tour of both Great Britain and the USA.

In December 1988, John Watson *(above left)*, a professional trombonist who had played with many big bands, went to New York to organise the licensing of a British Glenn Miller orchestra and to obtain permission to play the original scores and musical arrangements. The Glenn Miller (UK) Orchestra comprises five saxophones, four trumpets, four trombones, piano, drums and bass, making a 16-piece band in all, plus a male vocalist, Tony Mansell, and female singer, Jan Messeder. Just like the original band, an 'Uptown Hall Gang' has been created using several of the corner men from the orchestra, featuring the trumpet and vocals of Mike Lovatt and driving tenor sax of Johnnie Evans. These pictures were taken during the concert at the De Montfort Hall in Leicester on November 17, 1995 on the very same stage that Glenn had performed in 1944 (see page 65).

'Mostly we play the old songs', says John Watson. 'They age gracefully and mellow with the years. If anything, we honestly think the authentic Glenn Miller music today is more popular than ever before, and we owe it to Glenn to keep it that way.'

The Nuremberg soccer stadium where the band played on July 1, 1945 (see page 152). This stadium, and its believed reputation, was confused by the band with the nearby Zeppelinwiese, built by the Nazis for their monumental rallies.

Index

COMPILED BY PETER B. GUNN
Note: page numbers in *italics* refer to illustrations

159

GLENN MILLER

BORN MARCH 1, 1904, DIED DECEMBER 15, 1944